Hans H. Ørberg

LINGVA LATINA
PER SE ILLVSTRATA

Pars II
Roma Aeterna

Instructions

Part of the
LINGVA LATINA
PER SE ILLVSTRATA
series

For further information on the complete series and new titles,
visit www.hackettpublishing.com.

Lingua Latina per se illustrata Pars II
Instructions
© 2005 Hans Ørberg
Domus Latina, Skovvangen 7
DK-8500 Grenaa, Danimarca
Distributed by permission of Domus Latina by

Focus an imprint of
  Hackett Publishing Company, Inc.
  P.O. Box 44937
  Indianapolis, Indiana 46244-0937

  www.hackettpublishing.com

ISBN: 978-1-58510-055-2

All rights reserved
Printed in the United States of America.

20 19 18 17 16   9 10 11 12 13

LATINA PER SE ILLVSTRATA
PARS II: ROMA AETERNA

INSTRUCTIONS

Chapter 36

Part II of LINGVA LATINA PER SE ILLVSTRATA opens with a chapter on the Eternal City, *Rōma Aeterna*, as it looked in the 2nd century A.D. You read about its location on the banks of the Tiber on and around the Seven Hills, and about the splendid buildings and historic monuments found in the capital of the Roman Empire. The illustrations will give you an idea of what some of these monuments looked like in ancient times.

Rōma Aeterna, 'the Eternal City'

Posterity has not been kind to the remains of ancient Rome. Several medieval and Renaissance churches and palaces were built with materials taken from the ruins of ancient temples and public buildings. Nevertheless, some buildings have been preserved, because they were transformed into churches, e.g. the Senate-House, the *Cūria,* and the Temple of Faustina in the Forum. Here also the front row of columns of the temple of Saturn is still standing, as are a few columns of the Temple of Vespasian and the Temple of Castor. The temple of Vesta has been partly restored. The other Forum buildings mentioned in this chapter have all but disappeared: all that remains of most of them is their foundations.

The monuments of ancient Rome

Among the monuments elsewhere in the City that have been more or less preserved should be mentioned the Flavian Amphitheater, which was later named the Colosseum, the Arch of Titus with its reliefs showing Titus's triumph after the capture of Jerusalem, the Pantheon, a round temple with a huge dome, Trajan's column, which now bears a statue of Saint Peter, and the tomb of the Emperor Hadrian, which was converted into a medieval castle and called Castel Sant'Angelo. The best preserved Roman baths, those of Caracalla and Diocletian, were built in the 3rd century A.D., but ruins remain of the *thermae Trāiānī* on the Esquiline Hill above the Colosseum.

thermae, 'baths'

Sometimes inscriptions on the monuments give us some information of their origin and function, but it is only by combining the archaeological finds with the frequent references to localities in Rome found in Roman writers that we obtain factual knowledge about the topographical history of Rome. As far as most of the major buildings are concerned we know both when and by whom they were constructed, and we are familiar with a great many historical events that are connected with the individual monuments.

archaeology and literary sources

Be sure to make full use of the maps. There is a full map of ancient Rome on the inside of the cover, and detailed maps of the Forum and its surroundings on pp. 6 and 10. Here you will find all the names of buildings and localities mentioned in the text. The chronological survey on pp. 24-25 provides further support. The acquaintance with ancient Rome that you obtain by the study of this chapter will stand you in good stead in later chapters when you come to read about historical events that have taken place in and around the metropolis of the Roman world.

map of ancient Rome

chronological survey

no GRAMMATICA LATINA sections in cap. 36–47	As mentioned before, there are no more inflections for you to learn; for that reason you will find no GRAMMATICA LATINA section after each chapter until cap. 48. Instead these first chapters are devoted to a review of structures you have already learned; The solution of PENSVM A gives you a chance to review your Latin grammar beginning with some of the things you learned first, the declension of nouns and adjectives. But instead of sticking to one declension, we practice case forms of all five declensions with examples of the various functions of each case. This chapter focuses on the genitive. The ordinary *possessive* genitive appears along with the *partitive* and the *objective* genitives, the genitive of description and of value, and the genitive representing the *locative*. PENSVM B reviews the new words introduced in the chapter, and in PENSVM C there are questions about the content to be answered in simple Latin.
PENSVM A: review of grammar	
1. genitive	
PEMSVM B: new words PENSVM C: questions to be answered	

You have still a great deal to learn about *syntax*, i.e. the rules governing the application of the grammatical forms. You will also meet irregularities in the inflectional system. In this chapter note particularly:

dea, filia, plur. dat./abl *de__ābus__, fili__ābus__*	(1) The ending *-ābus* in dat./abl. plur. of *dea* and *filia* (ll. 40, 112, 160), which makes it possible to distinguish between the feminine and masculine;
magnificus -a -um comp. *magnific__entior__* sup.*magnific__entissimus__* *arduus* comp. *magis arduus* sup. *māximē arduus*	(2) the comparison of *magnificus:* comp. *magnific__entior__,* sup. *magnific__entissimus__* (ll. 19, 44, 245); the superlative *veterrimus* (l. 100) of *vetus* (stem *veter-*); and the use of *māximē* to form the superlative *māximē arduus* (l. 27): adjectives in *-eus, -ius* and *-uus* (except *-quus*) are compared with *magis* and *māximē*, e.g. *magis necessārius, māximē idōneus;*
~isse/≈us-a -um esse dīcitur/nārrātur	(3) the passives *dīcitur* and *nārrātur* with nom. + inf. perfect stating what is reported to have taken place, e.g. *Rōmulus Palātium mūn__īvisse__ dīcitur* (l. 12; more examples: ll. 66, 118, 148, 210, 268; cf. *putābātur* l. 222);
vēn-dere (act.) *vēn-īre -eunt* ('pass.')	(4) the verb *vēn-īre* serving as passive of *vēn-dere: vēneunt* (ll. 76, 178, 'are sold'); the two verbs are compounds of *īre* and *dare* with *vēnum*, 'for sale';
abl.(loc.): *terr__ā__ mar__ī__que*	(5) the ablative representing the <u>locative</u> in the phrase *terrā marīque* (l. 103);
dat. of <u>purpose</u>: *auxiliō venīre*	(6) the so-called <u>dative of purpose</u> (*datīvus fīnālis*) in *auxiliō venīre* (l. 140);
	(7) the <u>ablative of separation</u>: *domibus vacua* (l. 278) and *arc__e__ su__ā__* (l. 362);
cūrāre w. acc. + gerundive	(8) the use of the gerundive connected with the object of *cūrāre*. *Pompēius theātr__um__ aedifica__ndum__ cūrāvit* (l. 197) conveys roughly the same idea as *Pompēius cūrāvit ut theātrum aedificārētur:* the gerundive expresses what is to be done to something (cap. 31), in this case a theater; Pompey did not build it himself, but he provided for the theater to be built or 'had it built'. Cf. *vi__am__ Appi__am__ mūni__endam__ cūrāvit* (l. 254) and *nov__um__ for__um__ faci__endum__ cūrāvit* (l. 325). (Even with the verbs *dare* and *offerre* a gerundive may be added to the object, as in cap. 37, ll. 14 and 187: *arv__a__ col__enda__ dedit* and *s__ē__ videndam obtulit.*)
summus/medius/ īnfimus (mōns) = *summa /media/īnfima pars (montis)*	In an expression like *in mediō marī* the adjective *medius* denotes 'the middle of'. So *summus* and *īnfimus* may denote 'the top of' and 'the bottom of', e.g. *summum Iāniculum* (l. 26, 'the top of Janiculum'); *in īnfimō Capitōliō* (l. 55, 'at the foot of the Capitol'). Other examples: *in summā Arce, ad īnfimum Argīlētum, in summā Sacrā viā, in summā columnā* (ll. 53, 100, 171, 336).
gen. of description	The length of aqueducts is stated in the <u>genitive of description</u> (*genetīvus quālitātis*), e.g. *opus arcuātum pass__uum__ sexāgintā* (l. 257); ...*habet longitūdinem passuum quadrāgintā sex mīl__ium__ quadringent__ōrum__ sex* (ll. 260-261). In the expression *cum multitūdine omn__is__ generis pecudum ac ferārum* (l. 287) the genitive of description *omn__is__ generis* qualifies *pecudum ac ferārum*, which are <u>partitive</u> genitives.

Chapter 37

The introductory chapter on the city of Rome is now followed by an account of the history of Rome as told by the Romans themselves. The origins of Rome are lost in conjecture, so here poetic imagination has full scope. From a wish to link the prehistory of Rome with the city that had once fought so bravely against the Greek heroes arose the legend of the Trojan hero *Aenēās*, who after his flight from Troy and seven years' wanderings finally made his way to Latium, and there prepared the eventual foundation of Rome.

Roman history as told by the ancient Romans

Aeneas, progenitor of the Roman people

This theme was treated by the poet Vergil (*Pūblius Vergilius Marō*, 70–19 B.C.) in his famous poem the *Aeneid* (Latin *Aenēis*). As Vergil tells the story, Aeneas had been chosen by the gods themselves to lay the foundations of the later Roman Empire, as it had been prophesied in divine revelations.

Vergil's Aeneid

To a certain extent Vergil had the *Iliad* and the *Odyssey* of Homer as his models. The first six books *(librī)* of the Aeneid, where he tells of Aeneas's wanderings, are related to the Odyssey, which deals with the wanderings of Odysseus (Ulysses), and books VII–XII, in which the wars in Latium are described, can be compared with the Trojan War as described in the Iliad.

Vergil's models: the Iliad *and* Odyssey

Like its Greek models, the Aeneid is written in hexameters, the usual meter for epic poems in Greek and Latin. Since you are not yet able to read Vergil's verses in the original, we have made a prose version as close as possible to the wording and style of Vergil, and some important passages (printed in italics) have been left unchanged. This prose version of the first part of the Aeneid, which takes up the next four chapters, can form the basis for a later study of Vergil.

epic poem: hexameter

cap. 37–40: prose version of Aenēis *I–IV*

Chapter 37 corresponds with the 2nd book *(liber secundus)* of the Aeneid. It contains a description of the fall of Troy (*Trōia*) and the flight of Aeneas, as told by the hero himself to queen *Dīdō*, who offered him hospitality in Carthage (*Karthāgō* or *Carthāgō*). The chapter begins with a brief mention of the legendary kings of Latium from *Sāturnus* (whose reign was the so-called 'golden age': *'aetās aurea' quae vocātur*) to *Latīnus*. Then we are told how the Greeks succeeded in entering Troy hidden in a huge wooden horse, and about the heroic fight of the Trojans against the invaders. When king Priam (*Priamus*) is killed and the battle lost, Aeneas flees from the burning city with his old father *Anchīsēs*, his son *Ascanius* and his wife *Creūsa*. Although Creusa gets lost during the flight, the others reach a safe spot outside the city together with many other fugitives.

cap. 37: Aenēis *II*

The Greek name *Aenēās* follows the 1st declension in Latin: gen./dat. *Aenēae*, acc. *Aenēam*, abl. *Aenēā*. Of Greek men's names in *-ēs* some, e.g. *Anchīsēs*, follow the 1st declension (gen. *-ae*, but acc. with the Greek ending *-ēn*, abl. *-ā* or *-ē*), but most of them, e.g. *Herculēs, Achillēs, Ulixēs* (Greek *Hēraklēs, Achilleus, Odysseus*), follow the 3rd declension: gen. *-is* (acc. *-em* or *-ēn*); in the vocative these names end in *-ē*, whereas *Aenēās* has *-ā*.

Greek names in Latin:
nom. *-ās* *-ēs* *-ēs*
acc. *-am* *-ēn* *-em/-ēn*
gen. *-ae* *-ae* *-is*
dat. *-ae* *-ae* *-ī*
abl. *-ā*   *-ā/-ē* *-e*
voc. *-ā*   *-ē*   *-ē*

Aeneas was the son of Anchises and Venus; this is expressed with the participle *nātus* and an ablative (of separation, a so-called *ablātīvus orīginis*): he is *Anchīsā et Venere nātus* (l. 91) and is called *nāte deā* (l. 99):
    "*Heu, fuge, nāte deā, tēque hīs*" *ait* "*ēripe flammīs!*"
In this hexameter *hīs flammīs* is a more obvious ablative of separation. Cf. the ablative with *carēre* (l. 46) and *egēre*: *Iam nōn tēlīs egēmus* (l. 156).

ablātīvus orīginis: deā nātus

The dative mostly occurs with verbs; in this chapter notice the dative with *circum-dare*: *collō longa corpora sua circumdant* (l. 62, = *collum longīs corporibus* (abl.) *suīs circumdant*), and with *super-esse* ('survive'): *Nōlō urbī*

5

timēre + dat., 'be afraid <u>for</u>'	*capt<u>ae</u> superesse* (l. 198), and the dative of interest *filiō* and *patrī* with *timēre* (l. 247, Aeneas is not 'afraid *of*' but 'afraid *for*' his son and his father). Also some adjectives can be combined with a dative, as we have seen with *amīcus, inimīcus, necessārius, nōtus, ignōtus, grātus, proximus, cārus*. Now we find the dative with the adjectives *mātūrus* (l. 17), *benignus* (l. 37), *gravis* (l. 233), and *sacer* in cap. 38, l. 18. Note also the dative in the impersonal phrase *certum <u>mihi</u> est* + inf. expressing a person's determination to do something ('my mind is made up to...'): *Sī <u>tibi</u> certum est...* (ll. 204-205). *Plēnus* takes the genitive, as you know, or the ablative, e.g. *host<u>ibus</u> armāt<u>īs</u> <u>plēna</u>* (ll. 72-73; cf. ll. 25-26: *mīlit<u>ibus</u> armāt<u>īs</u> <u>complēvērunt</u>*).
adjectives + dat.	
original verses of the Aeneid	On p. 31 you read six original verses of the Aeneid (the figures in italics *42, 45, 49* indicate verse numbers in book II). As in Part I some help is offered in the margin: implied words are given in italics (e.g. *āvectōs esse, vōbīs nōtus est* Ulixēs?) and separated words are combined.
	In an account of past or 'historical' events the verbs are normally in the past tense or preterite (whether perfect, imperfect, or pluperfect). Ocasionally the <u>present</u> tense (the so-called <u>historic present</u>) is used in main clauses to make the description more vivid and dramatic, as in the story of the serpents attacking *Lāocoōn: natant, prōspiciunt, petunt, edunt*, etc. (ll. 56–66). In dependent clauses the preterite is common (l. 56: *Cum terram attig<u>issent</u>*; l. 61: *quī... ven<u>iēbat</u>*). – The conjunction *dum* generally takes the present, even if the main clause is in the preterite (see ll. 21, 41, 90, 201, 252, 279).
historic present	
temporal conjunctions: *ubi, ut, simul atque, postquam* + perf. ind.	We have already seen *ubi* as a temporal conjunction in the combination *ubi prīmum* (= *cum prīmum*); in this chapter it appears both in this combination (l. 34) and alone in the same function: *<u>Ubi</u> iam ad antīquam domum patriam perv<u>ēnit</u>...* (l. 193) and *Haec <u>ubi</u> dicta dedit...* (l. 276). The conjunction *ut* may be used in the same way (English 'as soon as', 'when'): *<u>ut</u> prīmum... hostēs in mediīs aedibus vīdit...* (l. 150, cf. cap. 38, l. 83: *<u>Ut</u> Aenēam cōnspexit...*). Like *simul atque* and *postquam* the temporal conjunctions *ubi* and *ut* are followed by the perfect indicative (not the pluperfect).
'cum' causāle + subj.	As we know, the conjunction *cum* is both temporal and causal. (1) As a <u>causal</u> conjunction *cum* is followed by the <u>subjunctive</u>, e.g. *Graecī enim, cum urbem vī expugnāre nōn poss<u>ent</u>, dolō ūsī sunt* (ll. 23-24) and *cum pariter fīliō patrīque tim<u>eat</u>* (l. 247). *Cum* in this function is called *'<u>cum</u>' causāle* (the English equivalent is 'as' or 'since').
	(2) As a <u>temporal</u> conjunction *cum* is followed by the <u>subjunctive</u> <u>imperfect</u> or <u>pluperfect</u> when we are told what took place at the same time as or previous to something else, as in this example: *<u>Cum iam sōl occid<u>isset</u> et nox obscūra terram teg<u>eret</u>, Trōiānī fessī somnō sē dedērunt* (l. 83). This *cum* (English 'when') is called *'<u>cum</u>' nārrātīvum*. In other temporal *cum*-clauses the verb is regularly in the <u>indicative</u> when a repeated action is concerned (*'<u>cum</u>' iterātīvum*, see cap. 29), and usually when the precise time of a single past event is stated (*'<u>cum</u>' temporāle*): see cap. 25, l. 53: *<u>cum</u> urbs... expugnā<u>ta est</u>*, and cap. 36, l. 148: *eō tempore... <u>cum</u> concordia omnium cīvium restitū<u>ta est</u>* (cf. *cum prīmum* + perf. ind.). In particular we find the present or perfect indicative in *cum*-clauses indicating a sudden occurrence, as we have seen in cap. 18, l. 128 (cf. cap. 27, l. 177 and 33, l. 113); in this chapter we read: *omnem domum gemitū complēbat, <u>cum</u> subitō mīrābile prōdigium <u>vīsum est</u>* (l. 219) and *Iam portīs appropinquābant..., <u>cum</u> Anchīsēs... <u>exclāmat</u>* (ll. 249-250). (This *cum* was called *'<u>cum</u>' inversum* by Roman grammarians, because they felt that it represented an inversion of an initial *cum*-clause, e.g. *cum omnem domum gemitū complē<u>ret</u>, subitō ... vīsum est*.)
cum' nārrātīvum + subj. imperf. or pluperf.	
'cum' iterātīvum + ind.	
'cum' temporāle + ind.	
'cum' inversum + ind. pres. or perf	

The noun *poena* denotes the penalty paid for an offence; the plural is used in the phrase *poenās dare* (+dative) which is equal to the passive *pūnīrī (ab...)*, e.g. *servus fugitīvus dominō poenās dat = servus fugitīvus ā dominō pūnītur.* In l. 68 you read *'Lāocoontem poenās meritās Minervae dedisse' dīcunt*: the words *poenās Minervae dedisse* are equivalent to *ā Minervā pūnītum esse.*

poenās dare, 'be punished'

Hecuba ends her summons to Priam to take refuge in the altar with these words: *Haec āra tuēbitur omnēs – aut moriēre simul!* Note here the ending *-re* instead of *-ris* in the 2nd person singular passive (*moriēre* is the future tense of the deponent verb *morī*).

2nd pers. sing. pass. *-re = -ris*

The indeclinable neuter *fās* denotes what is right by divine law, the will of the gods; it occurs mainly in the impersonal phrase *fās est* (ll. 238, 269, 'it is right/fitting').

fās n. indecl.

Chapter 38

This chapter is a prose version of book III of the Aeneid. Aeneas tells the story of his and his companions' dangerous voyage through the Aegean and Ionian Seas to Sicily. At the foot of Mount Etna (*Aetna*) they have a grim encounter with the Cyclops *Polyphēmus*, who shortly before had been blinded by Odysseus (*Ulixēs*). Aeneas ends his report with his faher's death and burial during the Trojans' brief sojourn in Sicily as the guests of king *Acestēs*.

cap. 38: *Aenēis* III

In antiquity navigation was suspended in winter. Aeneas spends the winter building a fleet of 20 ships (*classem vīgintī nāvium:* genitive of description), and he is not ready to sail (*ventīs vēla dare*, 'give sails to the winds') until *prīmā aestāte* ('in the early summer'): here *prīmus -a -um* is used in the sense of 'the first part of...' (cf. what you learned about *summus, medius, īnfimus* in cap. 36).

On his long journey Aeneas brought with him the Penates (*dī Penātēs*) of Troy – the name is used about the tutelary gods of a household, but also of a city. In a dream they tell Aeneas to depart from drought-stricken Crete and sail on to Italy, where a brilliant future awaits him and his descendantsin a new city. Aeneas informs his father of the matter: *patrem suum dē rē certiōrem facit* (l. 43); the same expression occurs in the passive in l. 79: *cum ā virō ipsō certior fierī cuperet, fierī* functioning as the passive of *facere*.

act. *certiōrem facere*
pass. *certior fierī*

The Latin ending *-us* (2nd decl.) corresponds to Greek *-os* (-ος): Greek names in *-os* therefore have *-us* in Latin and follow the 2nd declension, e.g. *Olympus, Rhodus, Ēpīrus, Daedalus, Īcarus, Priamus*, etc. Sometimes *-os* is retained in Latin, as we have seen in the names of some Greek islands: *Samos, Chios, Lesbos, Lēmnos, Tenedos;* in this chapter also *Dēlos* and *Zacynthos*. Here the Romans use the Greek accusative ending *-on*. Most names of islands, towns and countries ending in *-us* and *-os* are feminine: *Dēlō relictā* (l. 23).

Greek names in Latin
nom. *-us/-os   -a/-ē*
acc. *-um/-on -am/-ēn*
gen. *-ī   -ae/-ēs*
dat. *-ō   -ae*
abl. *-ō   -ā/-ē*

Ordinarily the Latin ending *-a* (1st decl.) corresponds to Greek *-ē* (-η), so Greek names in *-ē* get *-a* in Latin, e.g. *Eurōpa, Crēta, Ariadna, Helena;* but here, too, the Greek ending is retained in some names, e.g. *Samē, Andromachē* (these names also retain the Greek gen. in *-ēs* and acc. in *-ēn;* abl. *-ē*).

You have learned that the deponent verbs *ūtī* and *fruī* take the ablative (cap. 27 and 30). In this chapter you find two more deponent verbs with the ablative: *potīrī*, 'take possession of', with *aurō, rēgnō* and *Chāoniā* (ll. 14, 77, 95), and *vescī*, 'feed on', with *carne* and *sanguine* (l. 181).

dep. verbs + abl.: *ūtī, fruī, potīrī, vescī*

7

indirect questions: *sē, sibi, suus* referring to main verb	Aeneas's question *"Quae perīcula mihi vītanda sunt?"* is reported: *Aenēās... quaesīvit 'quae perīcula sibi vītanda essent?'* (ll. 101–103). This shows that in indirect questions, as in indirect commands, a reflexive pronoun refers to the subject of the main verb (the person asking). Another example: *Māter: "Cūr mē vocat fīlia mea?" Māter interrogat 'cūr sē vocet fīlia sua?'*
adjectives + gen.	Of adjectives that take the genitive you know *plēnus, cupidus* and *studiōsus*. Now you find the genitive with *potēns* ('powerful', 'having power over') and *ignārus* ('ignorant of'): *dī maris et terrae tempestātumque potentēs* (l. 141, a hexameter) and *ignārī viae* (l. 156). In cap. 39, l. 7 follows *memor* ('remembering', 'mindful of'): *memor veteris bellī*.
verbal nouns 4th decl.: ≈*us -ūs* m.	Instead of *postquam sōl occidit* and *antequam sōl ortus est* you find *post sōlis occāsum* and *ante sōlis ortum* (ll. 132-133 and 163); *occāsus -ūs* and *ortus -ūs* are 4th declension nouns formed from the supine stems of the verbs *occidere* and *orīrī*. In this way many verbal nouns are formed, e.g. *cantus* < *canere, cursus* < *currere, cāsus* < *cadere, exitus* < *exīre, rīsus* < *rīdēre, ductus* < *dūcere, gemitus* < *gemere, ululātus* < *ululāre, lūctus* < *lūgēre, flētus* < *flēre* (l. 169), and *versus* < *vertere* ('line', i.e. a 'turn' in writing).
quī- quae- quod- cumque	*"In quāscumque terrās mē abdūcite!"* cries the panic-stricken Greek on the Sicilian shore. When *-cumque* is added to *quī- quae- quod-* there is a choice of all possibilities: English 'any (no matter what)', 'whatever'. (Cf. cap. 39, ll. 104, 143: *quae-, quī-cumque es,* 'whoever you are'.) The desperate Greek concludes with the words: *Sī pereō, hominum manibus periisse iuvābit.* Here *iuvābit* is impersonal: 'it will delight/give pleasure' (so also in cap. 39, l. 82). – Another impersonal verb is *praestat* (l. 118), 'it is preferable/better.'
	The ending *-met* can be added to personal pronouns for emphasis. In this chapter you find *egomet* (l. 182), in the following *vōsmet* and *mēmet*.

Chapter 39

cap. 39: *Aenēis* I	It was the will of the gods that Aeneas should found a new kingdom in Italy, but not all the gods were favorably disposed. The goddess Juno hated all Trojans. The Trojan prince Paris, acting as judge in the beauty contest among the three goddesses Juno, Venus and Minerva, had wounded her by giving the prize to Venus. Furthermore she knew that the descendants of the Trojans were destined to destroy her favorite city, Carthage. Therefore she did her utmost to prevent Aeneas and his companions from reaching their goal. It became a hard undertaking, a huge effort (*mōlēs*) for Aeneas to lay the foundation of the Roman people – in Vergil's words:
Tantae mōlis erat Rōmānam condere gentem!
(*tantae mōlis* is *genetīvus quālitātis*, genitive of description).
	When the Trojans leave Sicily, Juno persuades *Aeolus*, ruler of the winds, to send a violent storm, which scatters the ships and drives them southward to the coast of Africa. Here Aeneas meets his mother, the goddess Venus, who shows him the way to Carthage. This city had just been founded by queen Dido, who had migrated from Tyre (*Tyrus*) in Phoenicia (*Phoenīcē*) after her husband had been murdered by her brother, the king of Tyre. Queen Dido gives the exiled Trojans a heroes' welcome in her new city and, deeply infatuated with their gallant commander, she questions him about the fate of Troy and about his adventures. This concludes the first book of the Aeneid, which is retold in this chapter.

We have seen the accusative in exclamations like *Heu mē miseram!* The acc. + inf. can be used in the same way: The wounded and vindictive goddess Juno, who has seen Minerva sink the ships of Ajax because he raped Cassandra in her temple, exclaims: *"Mēne rēgem Teucrōrum ab Italiā āvertere nōn posse?"* (ll. 16-17, 'Couldn't I...'). So Juno asks Aeolus to scatter Aeneas's fleet, promising him *Nympham suam fōrmā pulcherrimam* (l. 26); *fōrmā* is an ablative of respect: it answers the question 'in what respect?' The same phrase is used to describe queen Dido when she first makes her appearance (l. 193).

acc. + inf. in exclamations

ablative of respect

The queen is not alone, but *magnā iuvenum catervā comitāta*. Note the form *comitāta*, perfect participle of the deponent verb *comitārī*, here used in a passive sense with the ablative to mean 'accompanied by'; the same form is used about Aeneas leaving his companions *ūnō Achātē comitātus* (l. 95).

comitātus + abl., 'accompanied by'

In relative clauses the verb is normally in the indicative; but the subjunctive can be used to express cause or purpose. Examples: *dīs caelestibus cārus esse vidēris, quī ad urbem Karthāginem advēneris* (ll. 144-145, = *quoniam... advēnistī*, 'since you have come') and *praemittit Achātēn, quī Ascaniō haec nūntiet eumque in urbem dūcat* (ll. 263-264, = *ut Ascaniō haec nūntiet...*). The subjunctive is also found in a relative clause referring to a negative or interrogative pronoun, as in cap. 36, l. 363: *nīl nisi Rōmānum quod tueātur habet*.

relative clause w. subj. expressing cause or purpose

Instead of a statement in the superlative, such as *Aenēās omnium fortissimus fuit*, a negative expression with the comparative and the ablative of comparison can be used: *Aeneā nēmō fortior fuit* ('no one was braver than Aeneas'). This is common in relative clauses, e.g. in ll. 210-211: *Aenēās, quō nēmō iūstior fuit nec... fortior* (= *quī omnium iūstissimus fuit et fortissimus*); cf. cap. 40, l. 62: *Fāma, quā nōn aliud malum ūllum vēlōcius est*. − The ablative of comparison is also seen in the phrase *dictō citius* (l. 56, 'sooner than spoken'). − The parenthetic phrase *mīrābile dictū!* (l. 167) shows the 2nd supine *dictū* with the adjective *mīrābilis*.

abl. of comparison of rel. pron.: *quō nēmō -ior est* = *quī omnium -issimus est*

Ut may be an interrogative adverb (= *quōmodo*, e.g. *ut valēs?* 'how are you?'), chiefly in indirect questions explaining how something has happened − or just that it has happened, e.g. *Aenēās nārrāvit quae ipse vīderat: ut Graecī Trōiam īnsidiīs cēpissent atque incendissent, ut ipse... fūgisset et... errāvisset* (ll. 311–314).

ut...? = *quōmodo...?*
ut in indirect questions

Chapter 40

The main theme in book IV of the Aeneid is the love story of Dido and Aeneas. After the death of her husband Dido has sworn never to contract a new marriage *(coniugium)*, but now she tells her sister Anna that she has fallen in love with her noble guest. Anna urges her to forget her dead husband and obey the dictates of love. During a hunting expedition Dido and Aeneas seek shelter from the storm in a cave, where they are united by the design of Juno. The queen begins a relationship with Aeneas which she herself calls *coniugium*.

cap. 40: *Aenēis* IV

The rumor of this affair spreads rapidly among men and gods. When Jupiter hears that Aeneas is about to forget his divine mission, he sends Mercury to order him to sail: *"Nāviget!"* Aeneas makes secret preparations for departure, but Dido suspects mischief and begs him not to leave her. When he tries to explain that he is destined by the gods to seek a new homeland in Italy, she flies into a rage, and after violent reproaches and threats she retires without waiting for his reply. Aeneas makes his ships ready for sea, and when neither threats nor entreaties have any effect, Dido sees no alternative but to seek death. She tells her sister to build a pyre in the palace yard on the pretext of wanting to burn everything that reminds her of her faithless husband: his weapons, his clothes, his portrait, and their conjugal bed. By night, while Dido lies sleepless in her palace, Aeneas is ordered by Mercury to put to sea at once, and at dawn the queen sees the Trojan fleet leaving the harbor. She heaps reproaches on herself and invokes the Furies to take revenge on Aeneas and his descendants. Then she mounts the pyre, draws Aeneas's sword, and throws herself on it. Her last words on the pyre, taken from the close of the fourth book (verses 651–660), can be read on p. 80.

Books V and VI of the Aeneid are here treated summarily. From Carthage the Trojans sail to Sicily, and Aeneas celebrates the anniversary of his father's death with sacrifices and games. Meanwhile the Trojan women set fire to the ships, but the fire is extinguished by a rainstorm sent by Jupiter. Aeneas punishes the women by leaving most of them in Sicily when he sails on to Italy. In Campania he visits the Sibyl at Cumae. She takes him to the nether world, where he sees his dead father, who shows him the great Romans of the future from Romulus to Augustus. He ends with the famous words about the destiny of the Roman as ruler of the world:

Tū regere imperiō populōs, Rōmāne, mementō, etc.
(*mementō* is the future imperative of *meminisse*.)

quam, quālis, quantus, quot, quī quae quod...! in exclamations	In her infatuation with Aeneas Dido exclaims: "*Quālis hospes tēctīs nostrīs successit, quam nōbilis, quam fortis! ... quam ille fātīs iactātus est! Quae bella exhausta nārrābat!*" (ll. 7-10) and her sister prompts her saying: "*Quanta erit potentia Poenōrum, quanta glōria tua, soror, sī cum duce Trōiānōrum tē coniūnxeris!*" (ll. 29-30). Dido's despair is described in these words: *Quō tum dolōre Dīdō afficiēbātur! Quōs gemitūs dabat!* (ll. 156-157). The examples show that, besides *quam*, the interrogative pronouns and adjectives beginning with *qu-* may be used in <u>exclamations</u> (cf. cap. 26, l. 91 and cap. 37, l. 93).
dat. of interest + final dat.: *mihi cūrae est*	Marriages are the concern of Juno; she is the goddess *cui coniugia cūrae sunt* (l. 36). The <u>dative of purpose</u> (or <u>final dative</u>) *cūrae* is combined with the dative of interest to indicate 'to whom something is an object of care'. Cf. Dido's remark: *Putāsne eam rem dīs superīs cūrae esse?* (ll. 142-143).
impersonal passive of intransitive verbs: *ventum est pugnābātur, -ātum est tacendum est*	Aeneas and Dido decide to go hunting (*vēnātum īre:* 1st supine of deponent verb *vēnārī*); the text runs (l. 50): *Postquam in altōs montēs ventum est...* (instead of *vēnērunt*). Intransitive verbs, like *venīre, pugnāre, tacēre,* are <u>impersonal</u> when used in the passive; cf. *pugnātum esset* (cap. 33, l. 121) and *pugnābātur* (cap. 37, l. 135). So also in the gerundive, which is a passive form, e.g. *tacendum est* (cap. 31, l. 178).
the impersonal verbs *pudet, taedet, paenitet* + acc. and gen./inf.	The impersonal verbs *taedet* (expressing disgust) and *paenitet* (expressing regret) are construed like *pudet:* the person affected by the feeling is in the <u>accusative</u> and the cause is expressed by a <u>genitive</u> or an <u>infinitive</u>. When Aeneas deserts her, Dido feels disgust with life: *taedet eam vītae* (l. 167, = *taedet eam vīvere*); the Trojan women set fire to the ships when they were sick and tired of roaming about: *cum eās longī errōris taedēret* (ll. 281-282) and were left behind, although they already regretted their action: *quamquam eās iam factī suī paenitēbat* (l. 289). You met this verb in cap. 39, l. 212: *nec tē paenitēbit nōbīs auxilium tulisse* ('you will not regret...'), and in this chapter Aeneas tries to soothe the desperate queen with the words: *nec mē paenitēbit tuī meminisse* (l. 124).

As you know, *meminisse* takes the genitive: in the last example *tuī* is the genitive of *tū*. So also *miserērī* ('have pity on'): the miserable Dido exclaims (l. 112) *"miserēre meī!"* where *meī* is the genitive of *ego*. The personal pronouns *ego, tū, nōs, vōs* have no possessive genitive (as the possessive pronouns *meus, tuus, noster, vester* serve to denote possession), but the genitives *meī, tuī, nostrī, vestrī* are used with verbs that take the genitive. The same forms are used with nouns as objective genitive, e.g. *memoriam tuī* (l. 119, 'the memory of you') and *meī imāgō* (l. 257, 'a picture of me').

miserērī + gen.

nom.	gen.
ego	meī
tū	tuī
nōs	nostrī
vōs	vestrī

The adverb *quīn* (= *cūr nōn?*) with the 2nd person of the present indicative expresses a request or order, e.g. *quīn tacēs?* (= *tacē!*). When followed by an imperative, *quīn* is emphatic (= *age*), as when Dido bids herself: *Quīn morere, ut merita es!* (l. 197). Cf. the use of *quīn* for emphasis with *etiam* ('indeed'): *Quīn etiam hībernō tempore classem ōrnās* (l. 108, cf. cap. 37, l. 264: *quīn etiam clāmāre ausus est*). As a conjunction (meaning 'that') *quīn* occurs after negative expressions of doubt and is followed by the subjunctive, e.g. *Equidem nōn dubitō quīn deā nātus sit* (l. 8; really an amalgam of two sentences: *quīn deā nātus sit?* 'why shouldn't he be born of a goddess?' and *equidem nōn dubitō*, 'I am certainly not in doubt').

quīn + pres. ind. or imp.

quīn etiam

nōn dubitō quīn + subj.

Quid moror? Dido asks, *an dum frāter Pygmaliōn mea moenia dēstruat aut Iarbās... captam mē abdūcat?* (ll. 115–117) and later she asks for a short respite *(moram brevem) 'dum fortūna sē dolēre doceat!'* (l. 162). The conjunction *dum* with the subjunctive indicates what is expected or intended: 'until', 'long enough for...'

dum + subj.

Chapter 41

This and the following four chapters present the early history of Rome as recorded in the first 'book' of the great Roman historian *Titus Līvius*, called Livy in English, who lived in the time of the Emperor Augustus (59 B.C.– A.D. 17). In 142 'books' Livy treated the history of Rome from the foundation of the city – hence the title of his work *Ab urbe conditā* – down to his own time. Of this voluminous work only 35 books have survived. These books cover the earliest period until 293 B.C. (books I–X), the Second Punic War 218–201 B.C. (books XXI–XXX) and the subsequent period until 167 B.C. (books XXXI–XLV). The content of the lost books is known to us in broad outline through ancient summaries.

T. Līvius (Livy): *Ab urbe conditā* I–CXLII

extant books: I–X and XXI–XLV

Livy's first book deals with the foundation of Rome and the seven Roman kings from *Rōmulus* to *Tarquinius Superbus*, who was expelled from Rome in 509 B.C. In chapter 41 Livy's prose has been somewhat abridged and simplified, but even here many passages stand unaltered as Livy wrote them 2000 years ago. In the following chapters the text gets closer and closer to the original and from chapter 45, l. 222 there are no changes at all.

cap. 41–45: Livy I

Livy's account has been supplemented with extracts from Ovid (*Ovidius*), especially from the didactic poem *Fāstī* in which he goes through the Roman calendar and relates the legends connected with particular dates (e.g. the founding of Rome on April 21st).

Ovid, *Fāstī*

What the Romans related about the origin of their city has little to do with reality. Livy is fully aware of this, but his delight in the old legends is unmistakable. In his preface he says that if any people has the right to trace its origin to the war god Mars (the father of Romulus), it is the Roman people!

11

Livy begins his history with the arrival of Aeneas in Latium. He made peace with king Latinus, who gave him his daughter *Lāvīnia* in marriage. This provoked war with the neighboring king *Turnus*, who was engaged to marry Lavinia. Turnus allied himself with the Etruscans (*Etrūscī*), but he was defeated by Aeneas. Ascanius, the son of Aeneas, founded the city of *Alba Longa* and became the first of a line of Alban kings. One of these kings, *Numitor*, was dethroned by his brother *Amūlius*. When Numitor's daughter *Rea Silvia* bore twins, Amulius had them exposed in the Tiber, but the boys, *Rōmulus* and *Remus*, drifted ashore. They were found being nursed by a she-wolf. When grown up they killed Amulius and resolved to found a new city on the Tiber. An omen taken from the observation of the flight of birds (*auspicium*) seemed to favor Romulus, so he founded the city on the Palatine Hill. When Remus ridiculed his brother's work by leaping over the new walls, he was killed by Romulus. Finally Livy tells the story of Hercules killing *Cācus* for robbing his cattle. This story serves to explain the origin of the ancient *Āra Māxima* and the worship of the Greek god Hercules (Greek *Hēraklēs*) in Rome (see cap. 36, ll. 178–183).

As a supplement to Livy's account of Romulus and Remus you read the passage in Ovid's *Fāstī* (II.383–418), where the poet relates the story of the exposure of the twins and their miraculous rescue.

impersonal *cōnstat* + acc.+inf.	Although Livy is well aware that the story of Aeneas is mythical, he uses the phrase cōnstat Trōiā captā Aenēam... vēnisse (ll. 2-3). The impersonal expression *cōnstat* followed by acc. + inf. states a fact: 'it is certain', 'it is an established fact that...' – Also note the impersonal use of *convenīre* about an agreement between two: *inter frātrēs* convēnit *ut...* (l. 145), 'it was agreed between the brothers', 'the brothers agreed that...' That which is agreed upon may be the subject of *convenīre*, e.g. Pāx ita convēnerat ut Etruscīs Latīnīsque fluvius Albula, quem nunc Tiberim vocant, fīnis esset (ll. 66–68).
quem -um vocant = quī -us vocātur *-us ~isse dīcitur = -um ~isse dīcunt*	In the preceding example the 3rd person plural *vocant* is used in a general sense: 'they (: people) call' (cf. *ut āiunt*, cap. 24, l. 61); in fact quem nunc Tiberim vocant = quī nunc Tiberis vocātur. Similarly, instead of *Aenēās Trōiā vēnisse* dicitur/nārrātur it is possible to say *Aeneām Trōiā vēnisse* dicunt/nārrant.
verbal nouns in ≈*us -ūs* m. *iussū* + gen.	New verbal nouns in ≈*us -ūs* (4th decl.) formed from the supine stem are *discessus* < *discēdere*, *adventus* < *advenīre*, *partus* < *parere*, *vāgītus* < *vāgīre*. The verbal noun from *iubēre* is only found in the ablative *iussū* + gen., 'by order of...', e.g. *iussū rēgis* (l. 119; cf. *monitū* + gen.: cap. 42, l. 318).
potential subjunctive present	Livy is not sure whether Ascanius is the son of Lavinia or Creusa, so he says: *quis enim rem tam veterem prō certō affirmet?* (ll. 53-54), and Ovid gives expression to his wonder at the way the wolf treated the twins with the words: *quis crēdat puerīs nōn nocuisse feram?* (l. 228). The present subjunctive in these questions denotes possibility ('who might/could possibly...?') and is called potential subjunctive. Cf. Dido's question: *quis Trōiae nesciat urbem?* (cap. 39, l. 219). The potential subjunctive also occurs in conditional clauses, e.g. *sī ā prīmā orīgine repetēns labōrēs nostrōs nārrem, ante vesperum fīnem nōn faciam!* (cap. 39, l. 133–135, 'if I should...'). About the past
imperfect	the imperfect subjunctive is used, e.g. *hīc ubi nunc fora sunt lintrēs errāre vidērēs* (l. 207, 'you might have seen...'); [*eōs*] *sēnsisse putārēs* (l. 221, 'you would have thought...'). Here the 2nd person singular is used in a general sense ('you' = 'one').

12

Chapter 42

Once Romulus had secured his reign by laws and symbols of power, he increased the number of inhabitants by opening a place of refuge, *asȳlum,* for all kinds of immigrants. There was an influx of men of low rank, slaves as well as free men. The next problem for king Romulus was how to get wives for his new inhabitants. The neighboring peoples felt contempt for the Romans and banned intermarriage (*cōnūbium*) with them. But Romulus devised a ploy: he invited Rome's neighbors with their families to games in Rome, and in the middle of the show he gave a sign to the Roman men to carry off all the marriageable young women!

This outrage brought about Rome's first war with her neighbors. In the ensuing battle with the *Caenīnēnsēs* Romulus distinguished himself by killing the enemy king and carrying his armor to the Capitol as an offering to *Iuppiter Feretrius,* to whom he vowed a temple. His most dangerous opponents, however, were the Sabines (*Sabīnī*). With the help of the treacherous *Tarpēia* they managed to take the Capitol, the citadel of Rome, and from there they put the Roman army to flight; but Jupiter stayed the flight of the Romans when Romulus vowed him a temple at the foot of the Palatine Hill – the *templum Iovis Statōris* (see cap. 36, l. 172; *Stator* comes from *sistere* and can mean 'Stayer').

During the renewed struggle the Sabine women threw themselves between the opposing armies and persuaded their fathers and husbands to make peace. Romulus entered into an alliance with *Tatius,* the king of the Sabines. After a few years of joint rule king Tatius was killed in a riot. This caused Romulus little regret. He also waged successful wars with *Fidēnae,* whose army he ambushed, and with the Etruscan city of *Vēiī.*

Legend has it that Romulus suddenly disappeared in a violent storm while he was mustering his troops in the *Campus Mārtius.* The suspicious soldiers were told by the senators that he had been carried off to heaven and deified.

After a short *interrēgnum* the Sabine *Numa Pompilius* was chosen king of Rome, and his election was confirmed by *auspicia*. Unlike his warlike predecessor Numa entered upon peaceful reforms. He built the shrine of Janus (*Iānus*) and had it closed as a sign that Rome was at peace (see cap. 36, ll. 99–107). He rectified the calendar, giving the year 12 months instead of 10, and organized the worship of the gods.

In the first book of his poem *Ars amātōria* Ovid tells the story of the Rape of the Sabine Women (as an illustration of what a dangerous place the theater is for young women!). And in *Fāstī* (III.215–228) we are told how the same women clasping their babies rush between the warring Romans and Sabines.

Livy makes use of the legendary history of Rome in his attempt to explain the origin of a great many political and religious institutions. He makes Romulus establish a bodyguard of 12 *līctōrēs* as an explanation of the attendants who preceded the Roman consuls and other magistrates bearing the symbols of power, *fascēs* (rods) and *secūrēs* (axes). Romulus is also said to have instituted the offering of *spolia opīma* ('choice spoils'), i.e. the spoils taken by a Roman general from the enemy leader he had killed in battle, to Iuppiter Feretrius at his temple on the Capitoline. Several religious institutions are ascribed to the pious king Numa. An *augur* confirmed his election by *auspicia,* divination from the observation of birds; he founded new priesthoods, including the *virginēs Vestālēs,* priestesses of Vesta (see cap. 36, ll. 111–115), the *Saliī,* priests of Mars, and the *pontificēs,* who were in control of religious

---

The Roman kings:
(1) Romulus

(2) Numa Pompilius

Ovid, *Ars amātōria*

matters in Rome. The term *interrēgnum* was still used in Republican times about a period when Rome had no consuls.

cum... tum...

About two of Romulus's innovations it says: <u>cum</u> *vestem purpuream induit,* <u>tum</u> *līctōrēs duodecim sūmpsit, quī fascēs et secūrēs gerentēs rēgī anteīrent* (ll. 5–8). The conjunctions *cum... tum...* are used about two items underlining the second (cf. l. 160: *Movet rēs <u>cum</u> multitūdinem, <u>tum</u> ducēs*).

subj. in rel. clauses:
purpose
result

Note also the relative clause <u>quī</u>... *anteīrent*, where the subjunctive *anteīrent* expresses <u>purpose</u>, as in *lēgātōs... mīsit <u>quī</u> societātem... pet<u>e</u>rent* (ll. 24–26) and *Iānum... fēcit, <u>quī</u> apertus bellum clausus pācem esse indic<u>ā</u>ret* (ll. 306-307; cf. cap. 40, l. 245). In some relative clauses the subjunctive indicates <u>result</u> or <u>quality</u>, as in l. 17: *sōlī centum cīvēs nōbilēs erant <u>quī</u> senātōrēs creārī poss<u>e</u>nt* (virtually the same as *tam nōbilēs... ut... poss<u>e</u>nt*); cf. cap. 40, ll. 175-176: *invēnī ratiōnem, Anna, <u>quae</u> mihi redd<u>a</u>t eum*. After the adjective *dignus* such a relative clause is common, see ll. 276-277: *sī rēgem <u>dignum</u> <u>quī</u> secundus ab Rōmulō numer<u>ē</u>tur creāveritis*.

expression of <u>purpose</u>:
(1) *ut/nē* + subj.
(2) *quī* + subj.
(3) 1st supine
(4) *ad* + ger.
(5) ger. gen. + *causā*

Let us sum up the different ways of expressing <u>purpose</u> in Latin:
(1) an <u>*ut/nē*</u>-clause with the <u>subjunctive</u>, e.g. *lēgātōs mīsit <u>ut</u> pācem pet<u>e</u>rent* (see ll. 4-5, 10, 106-107, 108, 164, 214, 242-243, 329, 332, 341);
(2) a <u>relative clause</u> with <u>subjunctive</u>, e.g. *lēgātōs mīsit <u>quī</u> pācem pet<u>e</u>rent*;
(3) the <u>first supine</u>, e.g. *lēgātōs mīsit pācem pet<u>ī</u>tum* (see ll. 104 and 220);
(4) <u>*ad*</u> + <u>gerund/gerundive</u>, e.g. *lēgātos mīsit <u>ad</u> pācem pet<u>e</u>ndam* (see ll. 41-42 *<u>ad</u> rapi<u>e</u>ndās virginēs*, 161 *<u>ad</u> foedus faci<u>e</u>ndum*, 346 *<u>ad</u> turb<u>a</u>ndam omnium pācem*, and cap. 41, l. 8 *<u>ad</u> arc<u>e</u>ndam vim*); and
(5) <u>*causā*</u> + genitive of gerund/gerundive, e.g. *lēgātōs mīsit pācis pet<u>e</u>ndae <u>causā</u>* (= *pācem petendī causā*).

indefinite pronouns:
quī- quae- quod-libet
quī- quae- quod-vīs

In Romulus's asylum on the Capitoline Hill <u>any</u> person, *qu<u>ī</u>libet homō* (l. 13), could take refuge. The indefinite pronoun *quī- quae- quod-/quid-<u>libet</u>*, is formed from *quī* + the impersonal verb *libet*: 'who-/which-/whatever <u>you please</u>'. (The same sense can be conveyed by the pronoun *quī- quae- quod-/quid-<u>vīs</u>*, literally: 'who-/which-/whatever <u>you want</u>'.)

~ēre = ~ērunt

Instead of the ending ~*ērunt* in the perfect (3rd pers. plur.) you sometimes find the older form ~*ēre*, both in poetry and in prose. Book II of the Aeneid begins *Conticu<u>ē</u>re omnēs...* (cap. 39, l. 304). Livy affects this form, in this chapter we find *convēn<u>ē</u>re, necāv<u>ē</u>re, tenu<u>ē</u>re, subi<u>ē</u>re, restit<u>ē</u>re, ēripu<u>ē</u>re, redi<u>ē</u>re, audīv<u>ē</u>re* (ll. 34, 106, 114, 118, 135, 205, 210, 213), and in Ovid *timu<u>ē</u>re* and *prōcubu<u>ē</u>re* (ll. 364, 385). Other archaic forms are -*um* for -*ōrum*

-*um* = -*ōrum*
utī/utī = *ut*

in *de<u>um</u>*: Romulus invoking Jupiter says *pater de<u>um</u> hominumque* (l.128, cf. *X mīlia sēsterti<u>um</u>*), and *utī/utī* for *ut*; it is found mostly in elevated style, as in the augur's prayer: *Iuppiter pater..., <u>utī</u> tū signa nōbīs certa dēclārēs* (l. 300; cf. cap. 43, ll. 104, 124).

abl. abs. with perf. part.

In recounting a course of events the historian often has recourse to the ablative absolute with the perfect participle, e.g. *R<u>ē</u>bus dīvīn<u>īs</u> rīte fact<u>īs</u>...; Cīvit<u>ā</u>te ita auct<u>ā</u>...; Turbāt<u>ō</u> per metum lūdicr<u>ō</u>...; Duce hostium occīs<u>ō</u>...* (30 examples in this chapter). The perfect participle being a passive form, such locutions state what has/had been done (in English rendered by a clause beginning 'after...' or 'when...'). Elsewhere he uses the nominative of the <u>perfect participle of deponent verbs</u> (with active sense!) referring to the subject in order to tell what someone has/had done (or does/did): *ēgressus* (l. 192), *profectus* (l. 194), *exortī* (l. 199), *persecūtus* (l. 217), *locūtus* (l. 251), *ausī* (l. 287), *precātus* (l. 295), *potītus* (l. 303), *ratus* (l. 305, perf. part. of *rērī*). English here has the active, e.g. *persecūtus* 'having pursued' or 'after pursuing', *ausī* 'daring', *ratus* 'thinking' or 'as he thought'.

nom. with perf. part. of deponent verbs

The conjunction *priusquam/antequam* may be followed by the subjunctive to indicate what is anticipated, e.g. *Fidēnātēs... priusquam [urbs] tam valida esset quam futūra esse vidēbātur, properant bellum facere* (ll. 185-186); *prius paene quam Rōmulus equitēsque... circumagerent equōs, terga vertērunt* (ll. 202-203); *priusquam forēs portārum oppōnerentur, Rōmānī velut ūnō agmine in oppidum irrūpērunt* (l. 205-206). Cf. cap. 43, ll. 73, 108, 123.

priusquam/antequam + subjunctive

The verb *abstinēre* (intransitive: 'keep away/refrain from') takes the ablative of separation: *bellō quidem abstinuit* (ll. 179-180); *urbe validā mūrīs ac sitū ipsō mūnītā abstinuit* (ll. 217-218).

abstinēre + abl.

The adjective *similis* takes either the dative (*deō similis*, cap. 39, l. 237) or the genitive: *plūrēs Rōmulī quam Numae similēs rēgēs fore putābat* (ll. 327-328). Also *prūdēns* takes the genitive: *prūdentissimus iūris* (l. 283).

similis + dat./gen.

prūdēns + gen.

Chapter 43

The third Roman king, *Tullus Hostīlius,* was a warlike king, unlike his predecessor. He soon found a pretext for declaring war on Alba Longa, but before the decisive battle his Alban opponent, *Mettius Fūfētius* – under the influence of the danger threatening them both from the Etruscans – proposed that they should settle their dispute with a minimum of bloodshed. There happened to be triplets in both armies, and it was agreed that the three Roman triplets, the *Horātiī,* should fight with the three Albans, the *Cūriātiī.* Livy gives a dramatic description of this triple combat. After the first violent clashes only one Roman remained alive and unhurt facing three Albans who were more or less wounded. Horatius, the Roman soldier, seeing that he had no chance of holding his own against the other three, took to flight so as to separate his opponents, and with the wounded Albans following him at varying distances he turned round and killed them one by one.

(3) Tullus Hostilius

The triumphant Horatius then returned at the head of the jubilant Roman army, but in front of the Porta Capena he met his sister, who was betrothed to one of the Curiatii. Seeing her fiancé's coat on her brother's shoulder she burst into tears, whereupon Horatius ran his sword through his unpatriotic sister!

According to the law Horatius should have paid with his own life for this crime, but when the *duumvirī* appointed by the king had condemned him to the gallows for *perduelliō* (properly 'high treason' – here in a wider sense), he at once appealed (*prōvocāvit*) to the people. In the subsequent trial (*iūdicium*) he was acquitted, not least because his father defended him. Horatius' father even declared that his daughter had been justly killed!

Mettius, who was now subject to Rome, planned treason against his new masters. During a joint battle against the towns of Fidenae and Veii he moved his army away from the Romans, ready to join the enemy if they got the upper hand. But the Romans were victorious without Alban support, and Tullus took revenge. Mettius was put to death in a horrible way, and Alba Longa was destroyed and all its inhabitants moved to Rome. The population of Rome was doubled, and Mount Caelius was incorporated into the city. King Tullus Hostilius erected the first senate-house, which was named the *cūria Hostīlia* (it was pulled down by Julius Caesar, see cap. 36, ll. 82–84 and 96–98).

	Tullus also waged a successful war against the Sabines. Soon afterwards Rome was afflicted with the plague. When the king himself fell ill, he at last began worshiping the gods, but did not perform the religious rites properly. Jupiter struck him with lightning.
Cicero, *Dē inventiōne*	The chapter ends with a short extract from the earliest work of *M. Tullius Cicerō*, written about 85 B.C. It is the beginning of a textbook of rhetoric, *Dē inventiōne*, about the art of finding or devising the arguments and subject-matter of a speech. Here he takes the trial of Horatius as an example of a difficult case summarizing arguments on both sides.
sing. *uter, uterque* plur. *utrī, utrīque* adv. *utrimque*	The pronouns *uter* and *uterque* are used about two things or people taken separately. The expressions *uter populus* (l. 26) and *utrīusque populī* (l. 63) refer to each of the two peoples, Romans and Albans. Normally these pronouns are singular; when plural forms occur they refer to two groups of persons or things, 'both parties'. Such plurals are quite common in referring to two contending peoples. In the struggle between Romans and Albans the issue is <u>utrī utrīs</u> *imperent* (l. 64) and the description of the combat opens with the words: *Cum <u>utrīque</u> suōs adhortārentur* (l. 78) and ends: *<u>utrīque</u> suōs mortuōs sepeliunt* (l. 118, cf. l. 304). From *uterque* is formed the adverb *utrimque* ('from/on both sides'), e.g. <u>*Utrimque*</u> *lēgātī... missī sunt* (l. 13) and *bellum* <u>*utrimque*</u> *omnibus vīribus parābātur* (l. 29); this adverb occurs frequently when fighting is described, e.g. *īnstrūctī* <u>*utrimque*</u> *stābant* (l. 51); *Cōnsēderant* <u>*utrimque*</u> *prō castrīs duo exercitūs* (ll. 81-82). Note here the preposition *prō* meaning 'in front of', i.e. 'facing away from'.
facilis, difficilis, similis, dissimilis, gracilis, humilis: sup. *-illimus*	Like *facilis* and *difficilis* the adjectives *similis* and *dissimilis* form superlatives in *-illimus -a -um: cīvīlī bellī sim*<u>*illimum*</u> (l. 30); likewise *gracilis* and *humilis*: sup. *grac*<u>*illimus*</u> and *hum*<u>*illimus*</u>.
ablative of difference *tantō/eō, quantō/quō* + comparative: *quantō -ior, tantō -ior quō -ior, eō -ior*	We have seen the ablatives *multō* and *paulō* used before comparatives, e.g. *multō/paulō melior*, to indicate degree of difference. *Tantō* can be used in the same way: *tantō melior* ('so much the better'), often combined with *quantō*, e.g. *quantō longior, tantō melior* ('the longer the better'). Instead of *tantō* and *quantō* we often find *eō* and *quō*, e.g. <u>*quō propior*</u> *es,* <u>*eō magis*</u> *scīs* (l. 57, 'the nearer you are, the better you know') and <u>*eō māiōre*</u> *cum gaudiō quod prope metum rēs fuerat* (l. 117, 'with so much the greater joy as...'); cf. cap. 42, l. 144: *Ex equō tum Mettius pugnābat,* <u>*eō facilius*</u> *fuit eum pellere* and cap. 44, l. 143: <u>*eō magis*</u>.
<u>ablative of respect</u> <u>final dative</u> (of purpose) *spectāculō esse*	The <u>ablative of respect</u> can be used to indicate in what two parties differ, as in the expressions *numerō superiōrēs* (e.g. cap. 33, l. 144 and 37, l. 133). Of the two rulers Tullus *cum indole tum spē victōriae ferōcior erat* (ll. 65-66), the Horatii and Curiatii were *nec aetāte nec vīribus disparēs* (l. 69), but at the end of the combat Horatius and the wounded Curiatius were *nec spē nec vīribus parēs* (ll. 109-110, cf. cap. 44, l. 142 *glōriā pār*, 371 *disparēs mōribus*, 433 *et aetāte et vīribus validior*). Cf. *māiōrēs nātū* (l. 39, 'older'), where *nātū* is the ablative of a verbal noun from *nāscī* (as a matter of fact the 2nd supine in *-ū* is originally the ablative of respect of 4th declension verbal nouns). – The <u>final dative</u> or dative of purpose occurs in the phrase *spectāculō esse* (ll. 60 and 92, 'be displayed /in sight').
	For the sake of variation Latin writers sometimes replace an adjective-noun combination with an abstract noun combined with a genitive. Horatius Senior first refers to *tam dēfōrme spectāculum*, and later to *tanta* <u>*foeditās*</u> *suppliciī* (ll. 170 and 178); the description of Mettius's horrifying punishment ends: *Āvertēre omnēs ab tantā* <u>*foeditāte*</u> *spectāculī oculōs* (l. 265).

Chapter 44

This chapter deals with the three kings *Ancus Mārcius, Tarquinius Prīscus* and *Servius Tullius*. Important parts are also played by Tarquinius's arrogant queen *Tanaquīl* and Servius's cruel daughter *Tullia*, who became the last queen in Rome.

King Ancus Marcius, who was of a peaceful disposition like Numa, found himself compelled to declare war on the Latins (*Latīnī*) when they had made a raid on Roman territory and refused to return the loot. This event gives Livy an occasion to quote the old rules of law (the so-called *iūs fētiāle*) followed when restoration or compensation was demanded from the enemy (it was called *rēs repetere*). If the demand was denied, war was declared. The Senate had to be consulted: each of the senators was asked his opinion, *"Quid cēnsēs?"* (this consultation was called *sententiam rogāre*). War was declared by an envoy, a *fētiālis*, who threw a bloody lance into the enemy's territory.

(4) Ancus Marcius

Ancus conquered a couple of neighboring towns, moved their inhabitants to Rome, and settled them on the Aventine Hill. He is said to have built the prison, the *Carcer*, north of the Forum (see cap. 36, l. 154), and the first bridge over the Tiber, the *pōns Sublicius* ('the pile bridge').

Meanwhile *Lucumō*, a rich and powerful man from the Etruscan city of *Tarquiniī*, had moved to Rome in search of fortune with his ambitious wife Tanaquil. On their way an extraordinary augury had confirmed their expectation of a glorious future: an eagle carried off Lucumo's cap and put it back on his head! In Rome Lucumo, who called himself *Lūcius Tarquinius Prīscus*, won the favor of king Ancus. At the king's death he became guardian of his two minor sons. Before the election of the new king he sent the sons away, and so was chosen king of Rome.

King Tarquinius waged successful wars against the Latins and conquered several of their cities. After doubling his cavalry from 900 to 1800 men he defeated the Sabines and forced them to surrender the city of *Collātia*, where the king's nephew *Egerius* was made commander. In this connection Livy quotes the old formula pronounced at the surrender of a defeated enemy.

(5) Tarquinius Prīscus

After reigning for 38 years Tarquinius was murdered by order of Ancus's two slighted sons. At the instigation of Tarquinius's widow Tanaquil, the dead king's son-in-law Servius Tullius set himself up as king of Rome. This had been portended when, as a little boy, he was found asleep with his head burning!

King Servius Tullius has been credited with an important administrative reform: he divided the Roman people and the Roman army into 5 *classēs* on the basis of a statement of each citizen's property (*cēnsus*). The classes were divided into centuries (*centuriae*), 193 in all. In the popular assembly, the *comitia centuriāta*, in which laws were enacted and magistrates elected, votes were taken by centuries, giving the wealthier citizens the majority.

(6) Servius Tullius

Tarquinius Priscus's sons, *Lūcius* and *Arrūns*, refused to recognize their brother-in-law as lawful king. To appease them Servius gave them his two daughters in marriage; but the couples were unevenly matched, and soon the more hot-tempered of the two Tullias allied herself with the similarly disposed Lucius, and they had the other two put away. Tullia urged her new husband to seize power. He broke into the Senate-house and spoke out against the king. When king Servius appeared and protested against his son-in-law taking his seat, he was thrown out and soon after murdered.

Lucius's wife, the ferocious Tullia, was the first to salute her husband as the new king. When she was on her way home, her coachman suddenly stopped the carriage because he found the road blocked by the murdered king's body, but Tullia seized the reins and drove the carriage over her dead father!

Describing the 'handing down' (or 'tradition') of this outrage Livy employs the term *trāditur* ('is handed down', 'is reported') and in the same sense *fertur* (= *nārrātur*): *Foedum inhūmānumque inde trāditur scelus: Tullia per patris corpus carpentum ēgisse fertur* (ll. 445–447; cf. l. 227 *ferunt*, 'they report/relate', and l. 351 *fāma ferēbat*).

The crimes which began the reign of the last Roman king are described by Ovid in book VI of the *Fāstī*. An extract concludes chapter 44.

auxiliary verb *esse* omitted	The auxiliary verb *esse* is often omitted in the future infinitive and in the perfect infinitive passive, fx. *sē... habitūrum* (l. 21); *in novō populō... futūrum locum...* (l. 113); *Tatium... rēgem factum, et Numam... in rēgnum accītum* (ll. 149-150). In the 3rd person of the perfect passive *est, sunt* are apt to be left out by Livy, e.g. *Aventīnum novae multitūdinī datum* (l. 72); *quibus in valle Murciā datae sēdēs. Iāniculum quoque urbī adiectum* (l. 79); *totidem centuriae factae. Quīnta classis aucta* (l. 324), etc.
direct discourse ("...") indirect discourse ('...'): main clauses: acc.+inf. dependent clauses: subj.	Reporting what a person says, you can use either direct discourse ("..."), as Livy does when he quotes the words of the *fētiālis* (ll. 26–40), or indirect discourse ('...'). Latin writers are very fond of indirect discourse, which is characterized by the accusative and infinitive construction. However, in all subordinate clauses within such acc. + inf. constructions (e.g. relative clauses or causal clauses beginning with *quia, quod* or *quoniam*) the verbs are in the subjunctive. You have seen this in the report of Augustus's proud remark *'marmoream sē relinquere urbem, quam latericiam accēpisset'* (cap. 36, l. 229-230; direct discourse: *"marmoream relinquō urbem, quam latericiam accēpī"*). In this chapter Tanaquil's words to Lucumo are reported (ll.112–114): *'in novō populō, ubi omnis repentīna atque ex virtūte nōbilitās sit, futūrum locum fortī ac strēnuō virō'*, and Tarquinius's words to the people: *'Sē nōn rem novam petere, quia duo iam peregrīnī Rōmae rēgnāvissent'* (ll. 147-148, direct discourse: *"Nōn rem novam petō, quia duo... rēgnāvērunt"*); *'Māiōrem partem aetātis eius, quā cīvīlibus officiīs fungantur hominēs, sē Rōmae quam in vetere patriā vīxisse'* (ll. 152–154, direct discourse: *... quā cīvīlibus officiīs funguntur hominēs, Rōmae... vīxī"*).
dep. verbs + abl: *ūtī, fruī, fungī, potīrī, vescī*	In the last example the ablative *cīvīlibus officiīs* shows that the deponent verb *fungī fūnctum* takes the ablative; cf. ll. 285-286: *eum iūra datūrum esse aliīsque rēgis mūneribus fūnctūrum*. A total of five deponent verbs take the ablative: *ūtī, fruī, fungī, potīrī, vescī*.
quam prīmum, 'as soon as possible'	As *prīmum* is the superlative of *prius*, the phrase *quam prīmum* is an example of *quam* + superlative denoting the highest possible degree: 'as soon as possible': *Tarquinius postulābat ut quam prīmum comitia rēgī creandō fierent* (ll. 143-144). And *rēgī creandō* is dative of purpose with the gerundive (= *ad rēgem creandum*).
dative: *eī nōmen Serviō /Servius est*	*Egerius* was the name given to Lucumo's nephew because he was *egēns* ('indigent'): *puerō egentī...'Egeriō' nōmen datum est* (ll. 103-104); the dative *Egeriō* is provoked by the dative *puerō*. In king Tarquinius's palace there was a boy *cui Serviō Tulliō fuit nōmen* (l. 226): the dative *cui* provokes the dative *Serviō Tulliō*. In such cases the nominative is also possible.

The gods had the fortune of Servius at heart: *Ēvēnit facile quod dīs cordī esset* (*cordī* is a final dative or dative of purpose): *iuvenis ēvāsit vērē indolis rēgiae* (ll. 240-241). The genitive of description (*genetīvus quālitātis*) *indolis rēgiae* describes character, just like *iuvenis ārdentis animī* (l. 366) and *mītis ingeniī iuvenem* (l. 369). It is often interchangeable with the ablative of description, but the genitive is preferred when inherent qualities are concerned.

<small>genitive of description
iuvenis indolis rēgiae</small>

The accusative *secūrim* (l. 262) shows that *secūris* is a pure *i*-stem like *puppis* and *sitis:* sing. acc. *-im,* abl. *-ī* (see cap. 47, l. 69). So is *turris*.

<small>*puppis, secūris, sitis, turris:* acc. *-im,* abl. *-ī*</small>

The ablative absolute is widely used with the perfect participle (40 examples in this chapter), but also occurs frequently with the present participle, e.g. when stating during whose reign something happened: *Tullō/Ancō rēgnante* (ll. 13, 92); other examples: *Spernentibus Etrūscīs Lucumōnem* (l. 108); *ventōque iuvante* (l. 184); *necessitāte iam et ipsā cōgente ultima audēre* (l. 432, 'now that the very necessity compelled him to try his utmost').

<small>ablative absolute
with perf. part.
with pres. part.</small>

The tumult after the murder of Tarquinius made people wonder *quid reī esset* (l. 266); Servius, seeing his son-in-law taking his place, asks, *"Quid hoc reī est?"* (l. 424). The partitive genitive may depend on a neuter pronoun, as here *reī* depends on *quid* ('what sort of thing?'). Cf. *quidquid agrī* (l. 198), *id agrī* (cap. 42, l. 187), and cap. 45, l. 46 *id temporis* ('at this point of time'), 258 *quid salvī est...?*

<small>*quid reī?*
partitive genitive with neuter pronoun</small>

The name of the Etruscan town *Tarquiniī* is plural. Therefore the ablative *Tarquiniīs* means both 'from Tarquinii' (l. 93, abl. of separation) and 'at Tarquinii' (l. 95, locative). Sometimes Livy puts *ab* before a town name, e.g. *ab Tarquiniīs* (l. 111); *Nōn ab Corinthō nec ab Tarquiniīs* (l. 391) – the opposite of *Tarquiniōs aut Corinthum* (ll. 396-397).

<small>*Tarquiniī -ōrum* m. pl.</small>

A special function of the present infinitive appears on p. 149, where you read about the ambitious Tullia: *alterum Tarquinium admīrārī, 'eum virum esse' dīcere..., spernere sorōrem... nūllīs verbōrum contumēliīs parcere* (ll. 374–377), and *ab scelere ad aliud scelus spectāre mulier. Nec nocte nec interdiū virum conquiēscere patī* (483–485). Here the present infinitive has the force of the indicative (imperfect 3rd person). This is used in vivid narration and is called the historic infinitive. Stylistically it comes close to the historic present. More examples ll. 402–406 (and cap. 45, ll. 123, 124, 133, 136, 211, 240, 241).

<small>historic infinitive</small>

Chapter 45

Rome's last king, *Lūcius Tarquinius,* surnamed *Superbus* (*cui Superbō cognōmen datum est*), was a cruel tyrant who stopped at nothing to strengthen and expand his power. When the Latin *Turnus* dared to oppose him, the king had a large quantity of arms secretly hidden in his house; this was used as evidence in a false accusation of subversive activities, and he was condemned to death by his own countrymen. In this way the Latins were pacified.

<small>(7) Tarquinius Superbus</small>

The city of *Gabiī* continued to defy Roman power. Unable to take the city by force, Tarquinius devised a plan to seize it by treachery. His youngest son *Sextus* came to Gabii pretending to have escaped from his cruel father, and succeeded in winning the confidence of the inhabitants to such a degree that they chose him as their leader in the war with Rome. He now sent a messenger to his father asking how to make the most of his new power. Tarquinius gave no straightforward answer to the messenger, but walking with him in his garden he struck off the heads of the tallest poppies with his walking stick. When Sextus heard about this, he realized what his father wanted him to do: he killed or banished all the prominent Gabians, and then delivered the defenseless city to the Roman king!

After telling the story of the oracle which promised *Brūtus* supremacy in Rome because he alone understood its hidden meaning, Livy proceeds to tell the dramatic events which led to the expulsion of the royal family from Rome.

During the siege of the city of *Ardea* the king's three sons and *Collātīnus*, son of the king's cousin Egerius, started a quarrel about whose wife was the most virtuous. To decide the matter, they paid unannounced visits to their wives. Sextus Tarquinius was infatuated with the winner, Collatinus's beautiful wife *Lucrētia*, whom they found spinning wool in her home in Collatia. A few days later Sextus went to Collatia, entered Lucretia's chamber sword in hand, woke the sleeping woman and raped her. After his departure Lucretia sent for her husband and her father, who arrived together with Brutus. She told them what she had suffered, demanded vengeance, and thrust a knife into her heart. Brutus grasped the bloody knife and swore that he would drive out the king and his family from Rome. The people and the army sided with Brutus, the king was banished with his wife and his three sons, and Brutus and Collatinus are elected the first Roman consuls by the popular assembly (the *comitia centuriāta*). This is a historical event dated to the year 509 B.C.

The first consuls, 509:
L. Iūnius Brūtus
L. Tarquinius Collātīnus

This chapter ends with Ovid's description of these events in the second book of his *Fāstī*.

You have now finished Livy's first book. In the text that you have been reading departures from the original have become less and less noticeable, and from l. 222 in this chapter (*Muliebris certāminis laus...*) the text is unchanged. From now on all the passages from Roman authors are presented unchanged – apart from omissions.

from now on: original texts

In this chapter there are some examples of the gerund in the genitive or ablative with an object in the accusative: *mōrem... senātum cōnsulendī* (l. 16, 'the custom of consulting the Senate'); *auctorque armą capiendī* (l. 293, 'and who prompted them to take up arms'); *exspectandōque respōnsum fessus* (l. 144, 'and tired of waiting for an answer'); *āvertendō noxam* (l. 266, 'by turning away the guilt'). In most cases, however, the construction is altered so that the noun is in the genitive or ablative and the verb form, now a gerundive, agrees with the noun as an adjective, e.g. *vēndendā praedā* (ll. 94-95, = *vēndendō praedam*); *libīdō Lucrētiae stuprandae* (l. 226, = *libīdō Lucrētiam stuprandī*; cf. l. 185, gerund without an object: *cupīdō scīscitandī*). We have the same construction in the dative with the adjective *intentus: fundāmentīs templī iaciendīs... intentum* (l. 100) and *intentus perficiendō templō* (l. 160). After a preposition *(ad, dē, in)* only the construction with the gerundive is possible: *dē renovandō foedere* (ll.78-79); *ad forōs faciendōs cloācamque Māximam agendam* (ll. 166-167); *in fossās cloācāsque exhauriendās dēmersae* (ll. 311-312): 'submerged in the digging of ditches and sewers').

gerund + acc. (object)

gen./abl. + gerundive

dat. + gerundive

ad + acc. + gerundive
dē + abl. + gerundive
in + abl./acc. + gerundive

There are several examples of the ablative absolute with the present participle: *illō adiuvante* (l. 118); *sequente nūntiō* (ll. 141-142); *pōtantibus hīs* (ll. 208-209); *sōle parante* (l. 347); *exsecrantibus quācumque incēdēbat invocantibusque parentum Furiās virīs mulieribusque* (ll. 325-326, 'men and women cursing her wherever she walked and invoking the Furies who avenge parents'). We also find the ablative absolute with adjectives: *īnsciā multitūdine* (l. 130); *rē imperfectā* (l. 144); *īnsciō Collātīnō* (l. 230); *illīs lūctū occupātīs* (l. 275); and with nouns: *auctōribus patribus* (l. 8); *duce Brūtō* (l. 298).

abl. abs. with pres. part.

abl abs. with adj.

abl. abs. with noun

20

Before accusing Turnus, Tarquinius Superbus tells the Latins that his delay *'salūtī sibi atque illīs fuisse'* using the dative of purpose *salūtī* (l. 59, 'had been (to) the salvation of...'). After punishing Turnus it was not difficult for Tarquinius to persuade the Latins to submit to the Romans: *haud difficulter persuāsit Latīnīs...* (l. 79-80). The irregular adverb *difficulter* is formed from *difficilis*.

<small>dative of purpose: *salūtī esse*</small>

<small>*difficilis*, adv. *-culter*</small>

Note several examples of the impersonal passive of intransitive verbs in this chapter: *ventum est* (ll. 67, 184, 303), *reditum (est) inde Rōmam* (l. 197), *ex omnibus locīs urbis in forum curritur* (l. 302), *rēgnātum (est) Rōmae... annōs CCXLIV* (l. 340).

<small>passive of intransitive verbs</small>

The citizens of Gabii express the hope that the war 'will soon be transferred from Gabii to Rome': *'brevī futūrum ut ā portīs Gabīnīs sub Rōmāna moenia bellum trānsferātur'* (ll. 118-120). This construction, with an *ut*-clause (*ut... bellum trānsferātur*) as subject of the future infinitive *futūrum (esse)*, shows how to avoid the rare future infinitive passive ≈*um īrī; fore* is often substituted for *futūrum esse*: *'fore ut bellum trānsferātur'* = *'bellum trānslātum īrī'*.

<small>*futūrum esse/fore ut* + subj. = ≈*um īrī*</small>

When the oracle tells the king's two sons that *imperium summum Rōmae* will be given to the one who first kisses his mother, they decide to keep silent about it so that their brother Sextus would remain *ignārus respōnsī expersque imperiī* (l. 190). The adjectives *ignārus* ('ignorant of') and *expers* ('having no share in') take the genitive; so does *īnscius* (l. 350), synonym of *ignārus*, like its antonyms *perītus* and *prūdēns*. New examples of the genitive of description are: *dubiae fideī* (l. 140, 'of doubtful reliability'), *opera... labōris aliquantō māiōris* (l. 165, 'rather more laborious'), *ōrātiō... nēquāquam eius pectoris ingeniīque* (l. 306, 'by no means in keeping with the state of mind...') and *animī mātrōna virīlis* (l. 408, 'a woman of manly courage').

<small>adjectives + gen.: *ignārus, īnscius, perītus, prūdēns, expers*</small>

<small>genitive of desciption</small>

The 1st supine occurs with verbs of motion like *īre, venīre* and *mittere;* in this chapter you find *praedātum īret* (l. 128), *mittit scīscitātum* (l. 133) and *exsulātum iērunt* (l. 334); about a father giving his daughter in marriage the 1st supine of *nūbere* is used: *fīliam nūptum dat* (l. 24), because he sends her away from home.

<small>1st supine + verb of motion</small>

The impersonal phrase *opus est* takes the ablative about what is needed, as when Mettius tells Tullus *'opus esse colloquiō'* (cap. 43, ll. 46-47). Lucretia sends word to her husband and father *'ut cum singulīs fidēlibus amīcīs veniant; ita factō mātūrātōque opus esse...'* (l. 251). Here *opus esse* takes the ablative of the perfect participle of the verbs *fierī* and *mātūrāre*.

<small>*opus esse* + abl. (of perf. part.)</small>

Chapter 46

The Roman historian *Eutropius* was commissioned by the Emperor *Valēns* (A.D. 364-378) to write an abstract of Roman history, *Breviārium ab urbe conditā*. His style is extremely concise, without literary merit, but nonetheless a model of clarity. The extract in this chapter covers the time from the expulsion of the kings to the outbreak of the Second Punic War in 218 B.C. Eutropius has based this part of his history on a summary of Livy, and his main interest is the feats of arms (*rēs gestae*) of the Romans. He mentions in passing the civil strife (*sēditiō*) between the patricians (the Senate) and the plebeians (*plēbēiī* or *plēbs*, 'the common people') which led to the election of tribunes of the people (*tribūnī plēbis*) charged with the protection of the people against the consuls and senators.

<small>Eutropius, *Breviārium ab urbe conditā* I-X</small>

In this period of her history Rome conquered all of Italy south of the Apennines and made war on the great naval power of Carthage. They first subdued various neighboring peoples, including the northern Etruscans. *Camillus* captured their southernmost city, Veii, in 396 B.C. A few years later Gauls from northern Italy descended on Rome. The Roman army was defeated on the banks of the *Allia,* a tributary of the Tiber, and the Gauls occupied the city except for the Capitoline (390). After a long siege the Romans were rescued by Camillus, "the second founder of Rome."

In the following years the Romans repulsed new Gallic attacks. After this Rome's most dangerous enemies were the *Samnītēs,* who were defeated after long wars, and the Greeks in southern Italy. The Romans met with stubborn resistance from the city of *Tarentum,* whose Greek inhabitants appealed to king *Pyrrhus* of Epirus for help (280). After some costly victories (hence the phrase 'Pyrrhic victory') the king retired to Sicily. When he returned to the mainland he was defeated by the Romans, who were now the undisputed masters of Italy south of the Apennines.

1st Punic War 264–241   The conquest of southern Italy led to war with Carthage, the great power of the Western Mediterranean. The First Punic War lasted from 264–241 (the Carthaginians, *Carthāginiēnsēs,* coming from Phoenicia, are also called *Poenī,* adjective *Pūnicus -a -um*). *Gāius Duīlius* led a large Roman fleet to victory over the Carthaginians in 260. The war continued with varying success on land and at sea. The Roman general *Rēgulus* was taken prisoner in Africa by the Carthaginians. He was then sent to Rome with orders to persuade his countrymen to make peace with Carthage; instead he urged the Romans to fight on. He returned to Carthage, where he died under torture. In 241 a decisive sea battle was fought between the Roman and Carthaginian fleets of 300 and 400 ships respectively. The Romans were victorious, and the Carthaginians had to make peace and abandon Sicily.

In the following years the Romans also conquered Sardinia and Corsica, and in northern Italy they captured *Mediolānum* (Milan) from the Gauls. The victorious general *Mārcellus* killed the Gallic commander and carried his armor, the *spolia opīma,* in triumph to the Capitoline.

The chapter concludes with a quotation from book VI of the Aeneid: Anchises in the nether world describing the triumphant Marcellus to Aeneas.

Roman chronology   Roman chronology took the foundation of Rome as its point of departure.
a.u.c.   Dates are given in <u>ordinal numbers</u> (*annō -ēsimō...*) followed by *ab urbe con-*
a.C., p.C.   *ditā* (or *urbis conditae,* abbreviated *a.u.c.* or *u.c.*), e.g. *annō ducentēsimō quadrāgēsimō quīntō ab urbe conditā* (*annō CCXLV a.u.c.*), 'in the year 245 after the foundation of the city' (examples ll. 85, 95, 125, 288). The modern chronology *'annō Dominī'* (A.D.) only dates from the 6th century. The year 754 after the foundation of the city (*ab urbe conditā*) is the 1st year after the birth of Christ (*post Chrīstum nātum*). Until this year dates can be converted from ancient to modern chronology (from *a.u.c.* to B.C.) by subtracting the Roman date from 754 – for the time after Christ dates are converted by subtracting 753 from the Roman date. Accordingly the year 245 *a.u.c.* is 509 B.C. – the year the kings were expelled from Rome. After this year dates are
post rēgēs exāctōs   sometimes given with the words *post rēgēs exāctōs* (or *ab expulsīs rēgibus*), 'after the expulsion of the kings' (see ll. 8, 35, 41, 48), or by stating the
-ō -ō, -ō -ō cōnsulibus   names of the two consuls in the ablative absolute, e.g. *Ap. Claudiō (et) M. Fulviō cōnsulibus,* i.e. in 264 B.C. (l. 308, cf. ll. 67, 145, 194, etc.). In the margin dates are given *a.C.* = *ante Chrīstum,* B.C. (and *p.C.* = *post Chrīstum,* A.D.). In the INDICES pp. 7–11 there is a list of Roman consuls with dates

22

margin dates are given *a.C.* = *ante Chrīstum*, B.C. (and *p.C.* = *post Chrīstum*, A.D.). In the INDICES pp. 7–11 there is a list of Roman consuls with dates (*a.C.* and *u.c.*). After the list of consuls there is a list of the triumphs of Roman generals beginning with Romulus's triumph over the *Caenīnēnsēs*. Such lists, the so-called *Fāstī cōnsulārēs* and *triumphālēs*, were set up on marble tablets in the Forum; several fragments of them have been found (see the reproduction on the cover of the INDICES).

The consuls had no less authority than the kings, but the Romans tried to protect themselves against abuse of power by every year electing not one, but two new consuls. Only when the security of the State (*rēs pūblica*) was seriously endangered did they appoint a *dictātor*, who was given supreme power for a period of six months together with his subordinate, the *magister equitum* (see ll. 43–47, 80, 100, 104, 185). Under the consuls all important decisions were made in consultation with the Senate, whose members, *senātōrēs* or *patrēs*, were the heads of the noble patrician families. The consuls and other magistrates were elected from their number. Resolutions of the Senate are expressed by the phrase *(patribus) placet* followed by *ut/nē* + subjunctive (ll. 4, 12) or by acc. + inf. (l. 140, cf. cap. 42, l. 260).

The pluperfect passive is formed with the auxiliary verb *esse* in the imperfect, e.g. *laudātus erat/esset*. In late Latin, however, there is a tendency to put the auxiliary verb in the pluperfect: *laudātus fuerat/fuisset*. In Eutropius you find several examples of this: *fuerat expulsus* (l. 17), *datum fuerat* (l. 120), *datus fuisset* (l. 204); besides ll. 197, 350, 362, 394, 437; cf. l. 369 perf. *īnfrāctus fuit* for *īnfrāctus est*. Other peculiarities of late Latin are that *diēs* is always feminine (ll. 282, 388) and that *ipse* often stands for *is* or *ille* (ll. 104, 136, 138, 197, 205, 411). Otherwise the language of Eutropius agrees quite well with classical Latin. Some of his numerals are worth noticing: *decem et octō* for *duodēvīgintī* (ll. 343, 344), *octāvō decimō* for *duodēvīcēsimō* (ll. 56, 99) and *quadrāgintā novem* for *ūndēquīnquāgintā* (ll. 208-209).

≈us fuerat = ≈us erat
≈us fuisset = ≈us esset

The 300 *Fabiī* promise the senate '*per sē omne certāmen implendum (esse).*' Here the gerundive with *esse* understood functions as future infinitive passive; this is another way of avoiding the form ≈*um īrī*.

In PENSVM A we give you the choice between cardinals (*ūnus, duo, trēs..*), ordinals (*prīmus, secundus, tertius...*), distributive numerals (*singulī, bīnī, ternī...*) and numeral adverbs (*semel, bis, ter...*).

Chapter 47

This chapter is taken from a collection of essays (*commentāriī*) written by *Aulus Gellius* about A.D. 150 and published in 20 books under the strange title *Noctēs Atticae* (the explanation is that the writing was begun 'in the long winter nights in a country house in Attica'). The essays cover a great variety of subjects, linguistic, philosophical, legal, literary, etc., based on his extensive reading of Greek and Latin authors, whom he often quotes. Aulus Gellius has preserved many passages from lost works. This *commentārius* presents a chronological comparison of famous Greeks and Romans. Aulus Gellius observes that the illustrious Greek statesmen, philosophers and poets lived long before Rome became a great power, and that Greek art and literature flourished long before the first Roman literary works appeared.

Aulus Gellius, *Noctēs Atticae* I–XX

Most of the works of early Roman authors mentioned here are lost, except for some fragments, but 20 comedies by *Plautus* and 6 by *Terentius* (Terence) have been preserved. We also have a treatise *Dē agrī cultūrā* by *Catō*, which is the oldest surviving prose work in Latin.

Two short pieces from the same collection follow: one contains the story of the origin of the Sibylline Books (*librī Sibyllīnī*), the other some observations on the different oaths uttered by men and women (observations which are confirmed by usage in the comedies of Plautus and Terence).

gerund/gerundive -*und*- = -*end*-

The oldest Latin text mentioned by Aulus Gellius is *Lēgēs XII tabulārum*, 'The Laws of the Twelve Tables', which were written in 451–449 B.C. by a board of ten, *Decemvirī lēgibus scrībundīs creātī* (l. 61, cf. cap. 46, l. 88). The dative of purpose *lēgibus scrībundīs* (= *ad lēgēs scrībendās*) shows the old form of the gerund/gerundive with -*und*- instead of -*end*- in the 3rd and 4th conjugations (e.g. *gerere: gerundum* – hence the name *gerundium*; cf. *eundum* from *īre*); the same ending is retained in the old Latin phrase about the purpose of marrying: *līberum (= -ōrum) quaerundōrum causā*, 'to acquire children' (see ll. 154-155).

To describe the handing down of historical events A. Gellius uses *scrīptum relinquere* (ll. 23, 94), *(memoriae) trādere* (ll. 38, 42), *memoriae mandāre* (ll. 65, 96-97) and *prōdere* (l. 171). The impersonal verb *cōnstat* is here in the perfect: *cōnstitit* (ll. 18, 61, 190: 'it is established/an established fact'). The phrase *Nusquam scrīptum invenīre est* (l. 203) shows a peculiar use of the infinitive: 'is (to be) found'.

ablative of difference

The ablative indicating time occurs frequently in this text, not only the *ablātīvus temporis,* but also the so-called ablative of difference with *ante* and *post* stating 'how long before or after', e.g. *annīs post bellum Trōiānum plūs CLX, ante Rōmam autem conditam annīs circiter CLX* (ll. 22–26); *post* as an adverb (= *posteā*) is combined with *paucīs annīs* (ll. 52, 81, 107), *aliquot annīs/aliquantō* (ll. 98, 116) and *longō/brevī/aliquantō tempore* (ll. 84, 100, 109), and *posteā* with *multō* (l. 87), *magnō intervāllō* (l. 160) and *annīs paulō plūribus quam vīgintī* (l. 139; *paulō* + comp. is another ablative of difference).

lībra (pondō), pondō (327 g)

Lībra means (1) scales, balance (see cap. 13 top), and (2) a unit of weight: a Roman 'pound' (327 grams). 'Weight' is *pondus -eris*, 3rd decl. n., but it has a 2nd decl. ablative *pondō* ('in/by weight') which may be added to *lībra*, e.g. *decem pondō lībrae* ('10 pounds', l. 132: the possession of this amount of silver plate caused the ex-consul *P. Cornēlius Rūfīnus* to be banned from the senate by the censors); *pondō* is often used with the ellipsis of *lībrae* (see cap. 48, l. 863: *pondō CXXIII mīlia;* 'pound' comes from *pondō*).

euphemism

Like other languages Latin has many paraphrases, so-called euphemisms, for the idea of dying. Instead of *morī* we have seen phrases like *occidere, lūcem relinquere, ē vītā excēdere, dēcēdere,* and *exspīrāre*. In this chapter we find *obīre mortem/mortis diem* and *vītā fungī* (ll. 45, 114-115, 116). To 'sentence to death' is *capitis damnāre* (ll. 82, 92 and cap. 46, l. 190); here *damnāre* takes the genitive of the penalty (a construction that usually takes the ablative). Normally "juridical" verbs like *accūsāre, damnāre, condemnāre, absolvere* take the genitive of the charge, e.g. *fūrtī accūsāre, stuprī damnāre*.

gen. of the charge

Gellius begins by saying that he will limit himself to the time before the Second Punic War. So when he comes to mention writers who flourished after this war he says *prōgressī longius sumus*. Here the comparative *longius* means 'too far' (= *nimis longē*).

comparative: 'too ...'

Chapter 48

This long chapter contains extensive excerpts from Livy's description of the Second Punic War (218–201 B.C.). The outstanding Carthaginian leader in this war was *Hannibal*, who had sworn lifelong hostility to Rome.

Livy, Ab urbe conditā XXI–XXX

The direct cause of the war was Hannibal's attack on the Spanish city of *Saguntum*, Rome's ally. On hearing that the the city had fallen after a heroic defense, the Romans immediately declared war on Carthage (218). Hannibal then led a large army from Spain across the Pyrenees and the Alps to northern Italy, where he defeated the Romans in two battles. The following year he marched south across the Apennines and ambushed a Roman army at Lake Trasimene (*lacus Trasumennus*). After these serious reverses the Romans appointed *Fabius Māximus* dictator. Fabius harassed Hannibal's army, but avoided open battle. In 216 the consuls *Terentius Varrō* and *Aemilius Paulus* took the field against Hannibal at *Cannae*. Although numerically superior, the Romans suffered a shattering defeat: Paulus was killed with 50,000 Romans. After this the greater part of southern Italy went over to Hannibal.

Meanwhile the Romans defeated Hannibal's brother *Hasdrubal* in Spain, and in the following years fought with some success in Italy. Hasdrubal crossed the Alps with a new army to join forces with his brother, but was defeated and killed (207 B.C.). When the young Roman general *P. Cornēlius Scīpiō* succeeded in moving the war from Spain to Africa, the Carthaginians were forced to recall Hannibal. After his defeat at *Zama* in 202 Carthage was forced to make peace with Rome on severe terms.

In this chapter you read – with omissions, but no other changes – Livy's accounts of the siege of Saguntum and the declaration of war (from book 21), of the battle of Lake Trasimene and its repercussions in Rome (from book 22), of the battle of Cannae and the effect of the news in Carthage (from books 22 and 23) and finally of the recall of Hannibal and the conclusion of peace (from book 30). The summarizing passages in between are from the extant ancient abstracts (*Periochae*) of Livy's books supplemented with a passage from Eutropius.

Periochae, abstracts of the books of Livy

Fāma est is followed by the acc. + inf.: *Hannibale<u>m</u>... iūre iūrandō adāc<u>tum</u> (esse)* '...' (ll. 12–16, 'there is a story that Hannibal... was caused to take an oath that...'), which in turn is followed by the words of the oath in another acc. + inf.: '*sē, cum prīmum posset, hostem fore populō Rōmānō!*' In between we are told about Hannibal's young age (*annōrum fermē novem*), what he was doing (*blandientem patrī ut...*, 'coaxing his father to...') and what his father was doing (*cum... sacrificāret*), and about the formalities of the oath (*altāribus admōtum tāctīs sacrīs*).

fāma est + acc.+ inf.

The verb *referre* is used about submitting an issue for the deliberation of the Senate: *rem ad senātum referre* (l. 101) or *dē rē referre* (ll. 95-96). During the debate each senator is asked, "*Quid cēnsēs?*" (see cap. 44, l. 46), and he gives his opinion, *sententia*, by answering "*Cēnseō*" followed by the acc. + inf. with the gerundive, e.g. "*terrā marīque rem gerendam (esse) cēnseō.*" The final decision of the Senate is called *senātūs cōnsultum* (l. 679, here about the Carthaginian 'senate').

referre: rem/dē rē referre (ad senātum)

New examples of the <u>partitive genitive</u> with neuter pronouns are: <u>nihil</u> vēr<u>ī</u>, <u>nihil</u> sānct<u>ī</u> (l. 57), <u>quod</u> agr<u>ī</u> est (l. 280), <u>id</u> tantum host<u>ium</u> (l. 294), vīr<u>ium</u> <u>aliquid</u> (l. 496), nē <u>quid</u> sēri<u>ae</u> re<u>ī</u> (ll. 606-607), <u>quid</u> anim<u>ōrum</u> <u>quid</u>ve spe<u>ī</u> (ll. 670-671), <u>nihil</u> ultrā re<u>ī</u> (l. 779). Cf. host<u>ium</u> nimis <u>multum</u> (ll. 669-670) and ad <u>multum</u> di<u>ēī</u> (l. 544, 'till late in the day').

partitive genitive with neuter pronoun

25

distributive numerals with pluralia tantum: *bīna castra*	The distributive numerals are used with pluralia tantum (see cap. 33, l. 91); therefore *bīna castra* (ll. 421, 660, 766, 'two camps'). A collective singular is *hostis* for *hostēs*, which is common; besides we find *mīlitem* for *mīlitēs* (ll. 167, 796), *Rōmānus* for *Rōmānī* (l. 302), *Poenum* for *Poenōs* (419-420) and *equite* for *equitibus* (l. 532).
per- + adj. 'very ...'	The prefix *per-* before adjectives and adverbs has intensive force ('very ...'): *via perangusta* (l. 284), *ōrātiō perblanda* (l. 610; cf. the participles *permōtus, perterritus, perturbātus*); *prae-* in *praeclārus* and *praepotēns* has a similar function.
potential subjunctive	The potential subjunctive can be used to express oneself in a cautious and guarded way. Answering the Roman envoys the Carthaginian senator says *cēnseam* (l. 242, 'I should think') instead of *cēnseō*; and when provoked by Himilco Hanno says: *"Respondeam Himilcōnī..."* (l. 648, 'I might answer...') and *"velim seu Himilcō seu Māgō respondeat..."* (l. 665, 'I would like H. or M. to answer...'; cf. *scīre velim* l. 671). The imperfect of the potential subjunctive is used in this remark about young Hannibal: *haud facile discernerēs utrum imperātōrī an exercituī cārior esset* (l. 48, 'you could not easily have decided...') and about people's reaction to the news from the front: *variōs vultūs dīgredientium ab nūntiīs cernerēs* (l. 365, 'you would have seen different expressions on the faces of those walking away from the messengers').

Chapter 49

Cornelius Nepos, *Dē virīs illūstribus* Hannibal	The historian *Cornēlius Nepōs* (c. 100–c. 25 B.C.) wrote a chronicle of world history, of which only fragments survive quoted by Gellius (see cap. 47, ll. 25 and 37), and a collection of biographies, *Dē virīs illūstribus*. From this collection we still have the book dealing with foreign generals. The last biography in the book is that of *Hannibal*, which is reproduced in this chapter.
	Cornelius Nepos is not a very reliable historian. With your knowledge of events you can detect some inaccuracies in his report: he has Hannibal march on Rome immediately after the battle of Cannae and then tells of events that took place the previous year.
	We now learn what Hannibal did after his defeat at Zama. Under his competent leadership Carthage soon recovered, but when the Romans demanded his surrender, he took refuge with king *Antiochus III* of Syria. Hannibal encouraged the king to invade Italy, but Antiochus only sent an army to Greece, where he was beaten by the Romans (see next chapter). Hannibal fled to Crete and from there to king *Prūsiās* of *Bīthynia*. A delegation was sent from Rome to demand his surrender, but Hannibal escaped this humiliation by taking poison (183 or 182 B.C.).
	The concluding text is Livy's account of a conversation which Scipio is said to have had with Hannibal at Ephesus. This conversation never took place, but it presents an interesting portrait of the two great generals.
contractions (syncopated forms): *-v-* dropped before *-is-* and *-er-/-ēr-*	In verbs the *-v-* of the perfect is often dropped. This happens (1) before *-is-*, changing e.g. *-āvisse* to *-āsse* and *-īvisse* to *-iisse/-īsse*, and (2) before *-er-/-ēr-*, changing e.g. *-āverat* to *-ārat* and *-āverunt* to *-ārunt* (the complete rules are given after the chapter in the section GRAMMATICA LATINA). In Cornelius Nepos there are many examples of such contractions (called syncopated forms), e.g. *superārit* = *-āverit*, *commemorāsset* = *-āvisset*, *fugārat* = *-āverat*, *revocārunt* = *-āverunt*, *cōn-suērat* = *cōnsuēverat*. The last form is the pluperfect of the verb *cōnsuēscere -suēvisse*, 'get accustomed', the perfect of

which has present sense (*cōnsuēvit* = *solet*, 'is accustomed', 'is in the habit of') and the pluperfect has past sense (*cōnsuēverat* = *solēbat*, 'was accustomed'). Here we are told that Hannibal took poison *quod semper sēcum habēre cōnsuērat* (ll. 240-241). Cf. *nōscere*, 'get to know': the perfect *nōvit* means 'knows' and the pluperfect *nōverat (nōrat)* 'knew'.

In Africa Hannibal wanted to make temporary peace with Scipio; his purpose is expressed in the clause *quō valentior posteā congrederētur* (l. 112, 'in order that he could meet him afterward (so much) the stronger'): a relative clause of purpose (= *ut eō valentior...*).

quō + comp. + subj.: rel. purpose clause

The verb *dōnāre* is construed either like *dare* with dative and accusative, e.g. *Mēdus Lȳdiae ānulum dōnat*, or with ablative of the thing given and accusative of the recipient, e.g. *Mēdus Lȳdiam ānulō dōnat* (cf. English 'presents her with...'); the latter construction is used in the relative clause of purpose: *lēgātī Karthāginiēnsēs Rōmam vēnērunt, quī ... corōnā aureā eōs dōnārent* (l. 129). *Dōnāre* comes from the noun *dōnum*, which may be combined with *dare* in the phrase *dōnō dare* (= *dōnāre*), where *dōnō* is dative of purpose like *mūnerī* in the phrase *mūnerī dare* (l. 228).

aliquem rē dōnāre = *alicui rem dōnāre*

dōnō/mūnerī dare: dative of purpose

When envoys arrived from Rome Hannibal knew they had been sent *suī exposcendī grātiā* (l. 148, 'in order to demand him to be delivered up'). Like *causā*, *grātiā* takes an objective genitive, and *suī* is the genitive of *sē* (cf. *meī* and *tuī* as genitives of *ego* and *tū*). The same form recurs in l. 164: *sī suī fēcisset potestātem* ('if he had given (them) power over him').

sē, gen. *suī*

A command or request, expressed in direct discourse by the imperative, is rendered in indirect discourse by the subjunctive. Such an indirect command is usually preceded by verbs like *imperāvit/monuit/rogāvit ut/nē...*, but the subjunctive may stand alone. King Prusias tells the Roman ambassadors to seize Hannibal themselves: His words *"Ipsī, sī potestis, comprehendite (eum)!"* are reported: *'ipsī, sī possent, comprehenderent'* (ll. 225-226).

indirect command: subjunctive

Chapter 50

The victory over Carthage gave the Romans control of the Western Mediterranean. They now directed their attention to the East. In this chapter you read extracts from Livy's account of the conflict between Rome and the two great powers of the Eastern Mediterranean, *Macedonia* and *Syria*.

Livy, *Ab urbe conditā* XXXI-XLV

The Romans feared that king Philip (*Philippus*) V of Macedonia, who had supported Hannibal in the Second Punic War, would conquer all the free states of Greece and the kingdom of *Pergamum* in Asia Minor. To prevent this they declared war and sent an army to "liberate" Greece. After a few years' fighting the Romans, under *Flāminīnus*, won a decisive victory over Philip (197 B.C.), and during the Isthmian Games at Corinth the liberation of Greece was solemnly proclaimed. Only in 194, after conquering the insubordinate tyrant *Nabis* of Sparta, could Flamininus leave Greece with his army, and in Rome he celebrated a triumph lasting three days.

Philip V, king of Macedonia 221-179 B.C.

The next war was with king *Antiochus* III of Syria, who ruled a large kingdom in the Eastern Mediterranean including most of Asia Minor. Antiochus invaded Greece, where he was supported by the Aetolians, but was defeated by the Romans at *Thermopylae* in 191. The Roman consul *Acīlius* put an end to the war in Greece by capturing the heavily fortified city of *Hēraclēa* from the Aetolians. The Romans, commanded by *L. Cornēlius Scīpiō*, the brother

Antiochus III, king of Syria 223-187 B.C.

of Scipio Africanus, carried the war over to Asia Minor. With the support of king *Eumenēs* of Pergamum they defeated Antiochus in 190 and compelled him to give up Asia Minor west of Mount *Taurus*.

Perseus, king of Macedonia 179–168 B.C.

After the death of king Philip his son *Perseus* succeeded to the throne of Macedonia. The new king's aggressive policy brought about a new war with Rome, which lasted four years and ended with the final defeat of Perseus by *L. Aemilius Paulus* at the battle of *Pydna* in 168. Macedonia was now made a Roman province.

At the end of book 45 of his Roman history, the last that has been preserved, Livy tells of the events after the battle of Pydna: the arrival of the news in Rome, the capture of Perseus, and Aemilius Paulus's splendid triumph. A few days before and after this triumph the victorious general lost his two youngest sons, but he bore this terrible blow like a true Roman. In a public speech to the people he expressed his gratitude that the gods had seen fit to let the change of fortune that must follow upon such a great success overtake his family and not Rome.

In the GRAMMATICA LATINA section after this chapter there are examples of the same utterances in

indirect discourse:
acc. + inf. for main clauses
subjunctive in dependent clauses

(1) direct discourse, *ōrātiō rēcta*: *"Cūr flēs?" "Fleō, quia...; moriar, sī..."*; and
(2) indirect discourse, *ōrātiō oblīqua*. Here we find acc. + inf. for the main clauses (*'sē flēre...'* and *'sē moritūram esse...'*) except questions (and commands) which are put in the subjunctive (*'Cūr flēret?'*: indirect question; cf. indirect command p. 27). Dependent clauses within *ōrātiō oblīqua* are also put in the subjunctive (causal *quia... ēlūsisset*, relative *quem amāret*, concessive *etsī... dedisset*, conditional *sī abiisset*), and the 1st person pronouns *mē* and *mihi* become *sē* and *sibi*. Note especially the conditional *sī*-clause: Dido's words *"Moriar, sī abierit!"* are reported: *(Respondit Dīdō) 'sē moritūram esse, sī abiisset!'* The rule is that a future perfect in a dependent clause in direct discourse (here *abierit*) becomes the pluperfect subjunctive in indirect discourse (here *abiisset*). Example: *cum Macedonēs 'quodcumque senātus cēnsuisset id rēgem factūrum esse' dīcerent* (l. 31; cf. cap. 48, l. 751 and cap. 49, ll. 189, 199).

Greek ending *-as* (acc. plur.) = *-ēs*

Greek 3rd declension names sometimes retain the Greek ending *-as* (instead of Latin *-ēs*) in the accusative plural, e.g. *Magnētas* (l. 61), *Macedonas* (ll. 428, 535), *Arabas* (l. 521); cf. *Samnītas* (cap. 46, ll. 184, 189, 205, 207).

Chapter 51

Book 45 of Livy's *Ab urbe conditā* is the last to have survived. The hope of finding at least some of the remaining books has never been fulfilled. But instead of the full text we have brief summaries, so-called *Periochae*, of the content of the 142 books. In this chapter we reproduce extracts from the *Periochae* of books 48–61, which deal with the period from the Third Punic War (149–146 B.C.) to the death of *Gāius Gracchus* (121).

Periochae 48–61

P. Cornelius Scipio Aemiliānus 185–129 B.C.

The greatest figure in this period of Roman history is the son of Aemilius Paulus, *P. Cornēlius Scīpiō Aemiliānus*. He had been adopted by P. Cornelius Scipio, the son of Scipio Africanus, and in accordance with Roman custom he was given the name of his adoptive father with the second cognomen *Aemiliānus* after his real father. He was an outstanding general and statesman. When the Third Punic War broke out in 149 he served with distinction in Africa. In the following year he was elected consul although under the

Third Punic War 149–146 B.C.

normal age, and in 146 he conquered and destroyed Carthage. In the same year the Romans destroyed the rich Greek city of Corinth, the center of the Achaean League (*Concilium Achāicum*) which had rebelled against Rome. Scipio's last exploit was the conquest of *Numantia*, the capital of the *Celtibērī* in Spain, in 133. This put an end to organized resistance to the Romans in Spain.

During the following years internal conflicts emerged in Rome. There was popular discontent with the ruling class, the *nōbilitās* or *ōrdō senātōrius*, who had a monopoly of all public offices. This discontent was fostered by social problems resulting from the wars, which had dispossessed many Italian peasants of their land. *Tiberius* and *Gāius Gracchus* proposed agrarian reforms intended to provide land for the thousands of landless peasants who had come to Rome.

The Gracchi paid with their lives for their reform policy, but their work had a lasting effect on Roman politics. From then on the conservative senators, who called themselves *optimātēs*, 'the best', struggled with a strong reformist party, the so-called *populārēs*. At the end of the chapter you read an extract from the *Bellum Iugurthīnum* (see cap. 52) by Sallust (*Sallustius*); the historian gives his opinion of the political conflicts in Rome and the reasons for them. While Livy speaks in a censorious tone about the activities of the Gracchi, Sallust clearly shows his sympathy for the reformers.

Tiberius and Gaius Gracchus were closely connected with the family of the Scipios. Their mother, *Cornēlia*, was a daughter of Scipio Africanus, and their sister, *Semprōnia*, married Scipio Aemilianus. These family relations are shown in the genealogical table of the Scipio family on p. 294. The first ancestor is *Scīpiō Barbātus*, whose sarcophagus with a legible inscription is pictured at the beginning of the chapter. The language of the inscription differs considerably from classical Latin; the differences are explained in the margin. Note e.g. diphthongs instead of single vowels: *ei* for *ī* in VIRTVTEI, QVEI, and *ou* for *ū* in LOVCANA, ABDOVCIT; *ai* for *ae* in AIDILIS and CNAIVOD; in this last word we also see the archaic ablative ending *-ōd* which later became *-ō*.

early Latin:
ei, ou = *ī, ū*
ai = *ae*
-ōd = *-ō* (abl.)

Instead of *L. Mārcius M'. Mānīlius cōnsulēs Carthāginem obsidēre et oppugnāre coepērunt* you find the passive form: *Obsidērī oppugnārīque coepta est Carthāgō ā L. Mārciō M'. Mānīliō cōnsulibus* (ll. 44-45). With passive infinitives the perfect passive of *incipere*, here *coepta est*, is used in preference to the active *coepit -ērunt*.

act. *is rem agere coepit*
pass. *rēs agī coepta est*
  (coepit) *ab eō*

When studying Latin vocabulary it is easy to see how a great many words are derived from others. From now on each chapter is followed by a GRAMMATICA LATINA section on derivation or word-formation (*Dē vocābulīs faciendīs*). In cap. 51 it shows the formation of new verbs by means of prefixes (in Latin *praeverbia*). Most of these prefixes are prepositions, e.g. *ab-*, *ad-*, *dē-* and *con-* (= *cum*); *dis-* denotes separation or dispersal, and *re-* denotes movement back or repetition. Some prefixes are changed by assimilation before certain consonants (e.g. *ad-* to *af-* before *f*, *in-* and *con-* to *im-* and *com-* before *m* and *p*), and the addition of a prefix causes a change in the verbal stem of *a* to *i* or *e*, and of *e* to *i* (e.g. *ab-ripere* < *-rapere*, *ab-reptum* < *-raptum*, *re-tinēre* < *-tenēre*). The rules governing the changes are found in ll. 339-383; you will need to know them when doing PENSVM A.

derivation

prefixes
ad-, *ab-*, *dē-*, *con-* etc.

Chapter 52

Sallust, *Bellum Iugurthīnum*

The Roman historian Sallust, *C. Sallustius Crispus* (86–c. 34 B.C.) was on Caesar's side during the civil war between Caesar and Pompey. Caesar rewarded him by making him governor of *Numidia*. His knowledge of this province was useful to him in writing his *Bellum Iugurthīnum*, a description of the war which the Romans had to wage for six years (112–106) against the Numidian king Jugurtha (*Iugurtha*), the grandson of *Masinissa*. Chapter 52 contains excerpts from this work.

If Jugurtha was able to become a dangerous adversary of Rome, it was largely due to the incompetence and corruption of Roman politicians. Time after time Jugurtha succeeded in bribing influential Romans to comply with his demands. In this way he became absolute ruler of Numidia; when finally the Romans declared war, he bribed the consul *Calpurnius Bēstia* to cease hostilities. The disclosure of such corruption within the Senate aroused a storm of indignation in the Roman people. Jugurtha was summoned to Rome under safe conduct to give evidence, but he bribed one of the tribunes to forbid him to speak!

The first Roman commander to oppose Jugurtha effectively was *Q. Metellus;* but before winning a final victory, he was succeeded by *C. Marius*. Marius was a *novus homō* in Roman politics, i.e. the first man in his family to obtain high public office. Marius put an end to the war in Numidia, and with the help of his young staff officer *Sulla* caught Jugurtha in a trap. The king was taken to Rome to adorn Marius's triumph.

An opponent of the aristocratic senatorial government, Sallust emphasizes the inefficiency of the ruling class and the achievements of Marius during the Jugurthine war. He does not give an objective account of events.

archaisms:
uti = *ut*
quīs = *quibus*
foret = *esset*
duum = *duōrum*
huiusce = *huius*
-que... -que = *et... et*
~ēre = *~ērunt*
-undum = *-endum*

There are many archaisms in Sallust's work, e.g. *uti* for *ut* (ll. 26, 65 etc.), *quīs* for *quibus* (dat./abl. plur., ll. 177, 332, 647), *foret* for *esset* (ll. 285, 597), *duum* for *duōrum* (ll. 560, 662), *huiusce* for *huius* (ll. 5, 91, 477, 519) and *-que... -que* for *et... et* (ll. 97, 293, 500, 512, 679). In the perfect 3rd pers. plur. he prefers the original ending *~ēre* to *~ērunt* and in the gerund/gerundive he prefers *-und-* to *-end-* (e.g. *mittundum, subveniundum,* ll. 326, 327). The ablative of separation is used freely without the prepositions *ex, ab, dē,* not only with verbs like *expellere* (ll. 191, 596), *ēicere* (l. 192) and *prohibēre* (ll. 283-284), but also with *dēcēdere* (*Āfricā, Italiā,* ll. 246, 313, 366, 432), *ēgredī* (*Cūriā, castrīs, oppidō,* ll. 218, 557, 563) and *dēterrēre* (*proeliō,* l. 614).

final dative

The dative of purpose or final dative occurs in *dōnō dedit* (l. 15) and *praesidiō missum* (l. 653); also in *glōriae fore* (l. 33), *terrōrī esset* (l. 59), *gaudiō esse* (l. 78) and *lūdibriō habitus* (l. 408).

ablative of description

genitive of description

When describing a person's appearance or character Sallust seems to prefer the ablative of description to the genitive. Jugurtha is described as being *decōrā faciē* and *impigrō atque ācrī ingeniō* (l. 24, 53), Adherbal is described as *placidō ingeniō* (l. 253), Sulla as *animō ingentī* (l. 583) – and (with the genitive of description) *gentis patriciae nōbilis* (l. 581).

potīrī + abl./gen.

The deponent verb *potīrī*, 'become/be master of', usually takes the ablative, but in Sallust it takes the genitive: *fore uti sōlus imperiī Numidiae potīrētur* (l. 65); *postquam omnis Numidiae potiēbātur* (ll. 172-173).

quam + sup./*prīmum* ('as... as possible')

In this chapter you find several examples of *quam* before a superlative (with or without *potest*) denoting the highest possible degree: *quam māximās potest cōpiās armat* (ll. 164-165); *quam ōcissimē ad prōvinciam accēdat* (l. 336);

quam occultissimē potest (l. 560); *quam māximum silentium habērī iubet* (l. 618); *quam prīmum* (l. 592).

The impersonal verb *rē-ferre rē-tulisse* is a compound of *rē* (abl. of *rēs*) and *ferre: rē-fert* means 'it matters', 'it is of importance'; the person to whom it is of importance is expressed by a <u>genitive</u> or by *meā, tuā, suā...* (abl. fem. of poss. pron.), e.g. *quid id meā rēfert?* Sulla, who wants king Bocchus to surrender Jugurtha, tells him that what he promises is not gratifying to the Senate and the Roman people: 'he must do something that would seem <u>to be of more importance to them than to him</u>': *Faciundum eī aliquid quod illōrum magis quam suā rētulisse (: rēferre) vidērētur* (ll. 684-685).

rē-fert + gen./*meā, tuā, suā...*

The GRAMMATICA LATINA sections in this and the following chapters deal with <u>suffixes</u>, i.e. endings used to derive new words: verbs from nouns (cap. 52), adjectives from nouns (cap. 53), nouns from verbs (cap. 54), nouns from adjectives (cap. 55), and so-called <u>inchoative</u> verbs (cap. 56).

<u>suffixes</u>: derivational endings

Chapter 53

This chapter contains the part of Eutropius's history which deals with the years 105–67 B.C. In this period Rome was menaced by dangerous foreign enemies and weakened by internal dissension that finally ended in a bloody civil war. The great generals Marius, Sulla and Pompey (*Pompēius*) saved Rome from external enemies. In the years 102 and 101 Marius checked and defeated the advancing Germanic tribes of the *Cimbrī* and *Teutonēs*. In 90 a number of Italic peoples, who had been allies of Rome, started a revolt in order to obtain Roman citizenship; in this 'Social War' (*bellum sociāle*, from *socius*, 'ally') Sulla distinguished himself. He was therefore chosen by the senate to command the Roman army that was sent to fight Rome's new enemy, king *Mithridātēs* of *Pontus*, who had subjugated most of Asia Minor and Greece. However, the Roman people wanted Marius to be sent against Mithridates, so Sulla had first to march on Rome to oust Marius and his supporters. Then he crossed to Greece, where he defeated Mithridates in several battles; but before he had won the final victory, he made peace with Mithridates and returned with his army to Rome. The popular party had seized power during his absence, but Sulla crushed his opponents and took cruel revenge on them.

Eutropius V & VI.1–12

In this civil war young Pompey fought on Sulla's side and won such spectacular victories in Sicily and Africa that Sulla granted him a triumph in spite of his young age. In 76 Pompey went to Spain, where he helped to crush the rebellion of *Sertōrius*, a supporter of Marius who had offered strong resistance for several years. Returning from Spain in 71 Pompey conducted mopping-up operations after the Servile War (*Bellum servīle*) against *Spartacus*, the gladiator who had incited a large number of slaves to open warfare against their Roman masters.

In the meantime Mithridates had started a new war against Rome by occupying Bithynia, whose late king had bequeathed his kingdom to the Romans. The Roman general *Lūcullus* drove Mithridates out of Bithynia and even invaded his own kingdom of Pontus, so that he had to seek refuge with king *Tigrānēs* of *Armenia*, his son-in-law. Lucullus marched into Armenia and defeated Tigranes, but a mutiny among the troops he had left in Pontus prevented him from following up his victories. Mithridates launched a new offensive and regained Pontus. Lucullus was then recalled and superseded by *M'. Acīlius Glabriō* in 67 B.C.

In the same year Pompey was given the command of the war against the well-organized pirates who, in collusion with king Mithridates, made the whole Mediterranean unsafe and even threatened Rome's supply lines. Within a few months Pompey succeeded in ridding the seas of pirates (see Part I, cap. 32).

In 66 B.C., while Pompey was in *Cilicia* on the south coast of Asia Minor with his army, the tribune of the people, *C. Mānīlius,* proposed a law (*Lēx Mānīlia*) giving Pompey supreme command of the war against Mithridates. Among the speakers who pleaded for the law in the popular assembly were *C. Iūlius Caesar* and *M. Tullius Cicerō.*

This is the time when Cicero began to assert himself in Roman politics. The chapter ends with an extract from Cicero's work *Brūtus* or *Dē clārīs ōrātōribus,* in which he tells us about his training as an orator, his relations with other famous orators of the time, and his election as praetor for 66 – the year he made his great speech for Pompey – and as consul for the year 63.

-ennium '2/3/4/5 years'

-duum '2/3/4 days'

acc./abl. temporis

Latin has neuter nouns in -*ennium* to denote a number of years: *biennium, triennium, quadriennium, quīnquennium,* '2/3/4/5 years' (see ll. 45, 344, 393). Similarly the noun *bīduum* means 'two days', *trīduum* 'three days' (and *quadrīduum* 'four days'). Describing 'how long' something lasts these nouns are normally in the accusative (e.g. ll. 344, 393 and cap. 46, ll. 141,143), but in late Latin there is a tendency to use the ablative instead of the accusative to express time 'how long', e.g. *quadrienniō* (l. 45) and *trīduō* (l. 95). The ablative is also used to form adverbs in -*ō* from ordinals, where classical Latin prefers the accusative ending -*um: secundō, tertiō, quārtō, quīntō* (ll. 10, 12, 18), 'for the 2nd/3rd/4th/5th time' (= *iterum, tertium, quārtum, quīntum*).

ablative (locative)
tōtō..., tōtā...

We have seen the ablative (locative) without *in* denoting 'place where' in the phrase *terrā marīque* and with *locus: eō locō, multīs locīs* etc. Likewise the preposition is often missing in combinations with *tōtus* (and *cūnctus*), e.g *tōtā Asiā* (l. 358; cf. cap. 54, l. 36 *tōtā in Asiā,* 99 *cūnctā Asiā,* 332 *tōtō marī*).

Chapter 54

Cicero, *Dē imperiō Cn. Pompēiī*

This chapter contains the main part of Cicero's speech *Dē imperiō Cn. Pompēiī* (or *Prō lēge Mānīliā*), the speech which Cicero delivered in support of the law which gave Pompey the command of the Roman army in the war against king Mithridates.

After a short introduction, here omitted, Cicero gives a survey of the military situation in the East after the recall of Lucullus. He goes on to point out in what ways Rome's vital interests are at stake in the war. In the first place, the honor of the Roman people is involved, for Mithridates' murderous assault on Roman citizens must not remain unavenged. Secondly, Rome's Eastern allies, who are overrun or threatened to be overrun by the enemy, are eagerly hoping for Roman help. Thirdly the war has had serious consequences for the revenues of the Roman State, since it makes it impossibe to levy taxes (*vectīgālia*) in the richest of all the provinces of the Empire. Finally a large number of Roman citizens are threatened with economic ruin. Especially threatened are members of the equestrian order (*ōrdō equester*) including the *pūblicānī,* the provincial tax-collectors.

In the following section (*Dē magnitūdine bellī*) Cicero deals with the war situation in greater detail. He describes Lucullus's successful campaign and Mithridates' headlong flight. In carefully chosen words he alludes to the soldiers' failing discipline which has provoked the new enemy offensive and the defeat of the Roman army.

After evoking the seriousness of the situation, Cicero turns to the real issue: the appointment of a new commander in the war against Mithridates. He mentions the necessary qualifications of a great general and shows that Pompey possesses them all. This leads on to an unreserved eulogy of Pompey's brilliant achievements in all the wars he has fought, especially in the recent war against the pirates. Cicero concludes that Pompey is the only one who can win the war, especially since he happens to be stationed with a strong army near the theater of war.

There is no doubt that Cicero's admiration for Pompey's military ability was genuine. And indeed Pompey proved to be the right man for the task. The Lex Manilia was passed giving Pompey supreme command in the East; he defeated both Mithridates and Tigranes and extended Roman rule over vast new territories.

The Cicero text is followed by extracts from the extant summaries of books 100–102 of Livy. The subject is Pompey's great victories in the East, ending with the conquest of Jerusalem (*Hierosolyma*) in 63 B.C. In the same year Cicero, as consul, disclosed the conspiracy which Catiline (*Catilīna*) had organized in order to seize power in Rome. Catiline was forced to leave Rome, the leaders of the conspiracy were caught and executed, and the next year Catiline himself was killed in battle.
Periochae 100–102 on Pompey's Eastern campaign and the Catilinarian conspiracy

Finally there is an extract from Eutropius about Caesar's wars of conquest in Gaul (which he has described himself in his *Commentāriī dē bellō Gallicō*), about *Crassus*'s unsuccessful campaign against the Parthians (*Parthī*), and about the civil war between Caesar and Pompey. This civil war ended with Pompey's defeat in the battle of *Pharsālus* (48 B.C.) and his flight to Egypt, where he was killed.
Eutropius on Caesar's Gallic War, Crassus's Parthian campaign and the civil war between Caesar and Pompey

One of the devices used in Cicero's oratory is the <u>rhetorical question</u>, i.e. a formal question asked to produce an effect and not to be answered. When Cicero asks: *Quis igitur hōc homine scientior umquam aut fuit aut esse dēbuit?* (ll. 289-290) the obvious answer is: *Nēmō!* But no answer is expected; the rhetorical question is Cicero's way of saying that there never was a more knowledgeable man than Pompey. You will find many examples of rhetorical questions in this speech.
<u>rhetorical</u> question

At the beginning of his speech, when Cicero mentions the things that 'are involved' or 'at stake' in the war, he uses the passive of *agere*: *(bellum) in quō* <u>agitur</u> *populī Rōmānī glōria...;* <u>agitur</u> *salūs sociōrum...;* <u>aguntur</u> *certissima populī Rōmānī vectīgālia;* <u>aguntur</u> *bona multōrum cīvium, quibus est ā vōbīs ... cōnsulendum* (ll. 23–31; note here *cōnsulere* + dative meaning 'consult the interests of', 'take care of'; cf. l. 168); elsewhere he uses an impersonal construction with *dē*: *cum* <u>dē</u> *māximīs vestrīs vectīgālibus* <u>agātur</u> (l. 126).
rēs agitur/agitur dē rē

cōnsulere + dative ('take care of')

Cicero summarizes Pompey's short war against the pirates with these words: *tantum bellum... Cn. Pompēius* <u>extrēmā hieme</u> *apparāvit,* <u>ineunte vēre</u> *suscēpit,* <u>mediā aestāte</u> *cōnfēcit* (l. 372-373; cf. <u>extrēmā puerītiā</u> *mīles... fuit,* ll. 292-293). Here we see *extrēmus* and *medius* denoting 'the last/middle part of' a period of time (abl. 'at the end of...', 'in the middle of...'); *prīmus* can be used in the same way (*prīmā aestāte*, cap. 38, l. 3), but instead of *prīmō vēre* Cicero says *ineunte vēre*, using the ablative absolute with the present participle of *in-īre*, 'begin' (cf. *ineunte adulēscentiā*, l. 294).
prīmus/medius/extrēmus, 'the beginning/middle/end of'

ineunte... (abl. abs.), 'at the beginning of'

33

Chapter 55

After suppressing the Catilinarian conspiracy Cicero regarded himself as the savior of the Roman people. Nevertheless, his expectation of a brilliant political career as the leader who was to unite all good forces in defense of the established order was deeply disappointed. The optimates, fearing Catiline, had ensured his election as consul. But in the following years Cicero was pushed into the background, as Pompey came to an understanding with the leaders of the democratic party, Caesar and Crassus (the First Triumvirate, 60 B.C.),. Pompey and Caesar acquiesced when the tribune *P. Clōdius*, Cicero's bitter opponent, had him exiled in the spring of 58. After 18 months in exile he returned to Rome in 57. Cicero largely retired from public life and devoted himself to literary work. During the years 54–51 he wrote the *Dē rē pūblicā*, a treatise on political science. The last two chapters of ROMA AETERNA contain extracts from this work.

Cicero, *De rē pūblicā*

Dē rē pūblicā is a dialogue in 6 books modeled on Plato. Apart from the conclusion, *Somnium Scīpiōnis*, the work was lost until 1819, when most of books I and II and fragments of books III–V were found in a manuscript from c. A.D. 400, a so-called palimpsest, in which the original Cicero text had been painted over so that a text by Augustine (his commentary on the Psalms) could be written in its place. A page from this manuscript is reproduced on the back cover of this book, where the Augustine text can be seen under the original two columns of Cicero's text. The Augustine text has been removed from the column shown on p. 386.

In chapter 55 you read extracts from books I and II of *Dē rē pūblicā*. It is a dialogue between Scipio Aemilianus and some of his friends who arrive at his country house during the *fēriae Latīnae*, a religious holiday, in 129 B.C. Immediately after this holiday Scipio was found dead in his bed (see cap. 51, ll. 251–253). It was widely held that he had been murdered at the instigation of his brother-in-law C. Gracchus, whose reform efforts he had opposed. This turbulent political situation is the background for Cicero's dialogue.

After a preliminary discussion about astronomy, Scipio's learned friend *C. Laelius* raises the question of how to unite the conflicting parties in Rome. He asks Scipio to set out his ideas about the best form of government.

Scipio begins with a definition of *'rēs pūblica'*, and goes on to discuss the three forms of government: *rēgnum, cīvitās optimātium* and *cīvitās populāris* (Cicero's translation of the Greek terms *monarchía, aristocratía* and *dēmocratía*). As serious objections can be raised to each of the forms, he advocates a combination of the three. The excellence of the Roman republic derives from this combination.

In book II Scipio describes the development of Rome from earliest times. This selection includes his account of the first two kings, Romulus and Numa, and his presentation of Tarquinius Superbus as an illustration of the degeneration of monarchy into tyranny.

The discussion continues for two days (books III–VI). Recovered fragments and references in later authors show that they discussed the qualities of the ideal statesman (*rēctor reī pūblicae*) and the honors and rewards that await him. Scipio then relates a strange dream he has had twenty years before. The dialogue ends with this dream, the *Somnium Scīpiōnis* (see cap. 56).

velle + subjunctive

The verb *velle* is often followed by the subjunctive (without *ut/nē*), as *Vīsne igitur hoc prīmum... videāmus...?* (l. 31) and *Quam vellem Panaetium nostrum nōbīscum habērēmus!* (ll. 35-36, = *utinam... habērēmus!*).

34

Besides *audēre* (see cap. 31, l. 169) two more 2nd conjugation verbs are semi-deponent: *solēre solitum esse* (l. 150) and *gaudēre gavīsum esse; placēre*, used impersonally, may be semideponent: *placitum est = placuit* (l. 74;. cf. *placitus*, 'pleasing', cap. 40, l. 24). Another semideponent verb is *(cōn)fīdere -fīsum esse* (see cap. 52, l. 345 *cōnfīsī*).

semideponent verbs:
audēre ausum esse
solēre solitum esse
gaudēre gavīsum esse
(cōn)fīdere fīsum esse

Chapter 56

The *Somnium Scīpiōnis* has been preserved in full because it was separately transcribed and annotated. Scipio tells about his visit to king Masinissa of Numidia during the Third Punic War. The ninety-year-old king entertained his Roman visitor with stories about his famous grandfather, Scipio Africanus Major, whom he remembered from the Second Punic War. After this conversation Scipio dreamed the following night that his grandfather appeared before him among the heavenly stars, and spoke to him about the great deeds he was to perform for his country and about the reward awaiting him in heaven. Scipio's dead father, Aemilius Paulus, also stepped forward and spoke admonitory words to his son. The grandfather went on to describe the structure of the universe – the immovable earth surrounded by eight revolving spheres – and the music of the spheres, which the human ear cannot perceive. He pointed out the five zones of the globe, only two of which are habitable. He put forward evidence for the immortality of the soul (taken from Plato's *Phaedrus*) and concluded with an exhortation to use one's immortal soul in the service of one's country.

Somnium Scīpiōnis
(Dē rē pūblicā VI)

As an appendix, the Cicero text is followed by an Ode, i.e. a lyric poem, by Horace (*Q. Horātius Flaccus*, 65–8 B.C.). Guiltlessness is a safeguard against all dangrs, the poet solemnly declares. He illustrates this maxim with an incident that happened while he was strolling in the woods and singing about his beloved *Lalagē:* a formidable wolf turned away and fled! The poem concludes that he will always love Lalage wherever he may travel.

Horace, Odes
(Carmina)

Horace's models are the Greek lyric poets Alcaeus (*Alkaios*) and Pindar (*Píndaros*). The meter in the present poem is called Sapphic after the Greek poetess *Sapphō*. In the GRAMMATICA LATINA section there is an explanation of the meter and the division of the poem into four-line stanzas (*strophae*).

the Sapphic stanza

The subjunctive may be used with *oportet* and *necesse est* instead of the acc. + inf., e.g. *Hīc tū... ostendās oportēbit...* (l. 46, = *tē ostendere o.;* cf. ll. 239-240 and cap. 55, l. 26); ...*vīvendī fīnem habeat necesse est* (ll. 263-264, cf. ll. 275-276).

oportet, necesse est
+ subjunctive

The verb *quaesō* (1st pers. sing. pres. ind.) is used in combination with a request or a question: 'I ask you', 'please (tell me)': *St! quaesō* (l. 58, cf. ll. 81, 115 and cap. 50, l. 630).

quaesō

When discussing the vanity of posthumous fame Scipio asks: *Quid autem interest ab iīs quī posteā nāscentur sermōnem fore dē tē?* (ll. 214-215). The impersonal verb *inter-est*, 'it makes a difference', 'it is of interest/importance', is construed like *rē-fert* (with gen. or *meā, tuā, suā*...), e.g. *meā māximē interest tē valēre*. (In the example above *tuā* may be understood: *Quid autem tuā interest...?*)

interest impers. (+ gen. /*meā, tuā*...)

In Horace's poem note the peculiar use of the genitive in the first line: *integer vītae* (cf. 'integrity') and *sceleris pūrus* ('pure of crime', 'guiltless'). – In the last stanza the neuter form *dulce* is used as an adverb (= *dulciter;* cf. *facile*).

35

INDEX
(Numbers refer to pages)

A

ab before town name 19
ablative: absolute 14, 19, 20; comparison 9; description 30; difference 24; location 4, 32; respect 9, 16; separation 4, 5, 15, 30; w. verbs: *opus est* 21, *egēre* 5, *potīrī, vescī* 7, *fungī* 18, *dōnāre* 27, *nātus* 5, *comitātus* 9
-ābus dat./abl. pl. f. 4
accusative: w. *taedet, paenitet* 10; acc. + inf. 18, 28; in exclamations 9
agitur (dē) 33
annō -ēsimō a.u.c. 22
antequam + subj. 15
archaisms 14, 29, 30

C

causā + gen. 14
cause 9
certiōrem facere, certior fierī 7
certum mihi est + inf. 6
chronology (a.u.c., a.C.) 22
coeptus est w. pass inf. 29
comitātus + abl. 9
comparative: 'too ...' 24
comparison: *magis, māximē -eus/-ius/-uus* 4
cōnstat impers. + acc + inf. 12, 24
cōnsuēvisse 26-27
cōnsulere + dative 33
cōnsulibus, ..., abl. abs. 22
contraction 26
convenit impers. 12
cum +subj.: *causāle, nārrātīvum* 6; + ind.: *iterātīvum, temporāle, inversum* 6
cum... tum... 14
-cumque 8
cūrāre + gerundive 4

D

damnāre + gen. 24
dative: interest 10; purpose /final 4, 10, 16, 18, 20, 24, 27, 30; *eī nōmen Serviō est* 18; w. verbs: *circumdare, superesse* 5, *timēre* 6; *cōnsulere* 33; w. adj.s 6; *similis* 15
dea, dat./abl. pl. *-ābus* 4
deponent vb.s + abl. 7, 18; perf.part. 14
derivation 29, 31
dīcitur/nārrātur 4
difficilis, sup. *-illimus* 16, adv. *difficulter* 20
dignus quī + subj. 14
dōnāre + abl. 27
dum + pres. ind. 6; + subj. 11
-duum '2/3/4 days' 32

E

egēre + abl. 5
-ennium '2/3/4/5 years' 32

eō + comp. 16
~ēre = ~ērunt 14, 30
esse auxiliary omitted 18
euphemism 24
exclamations: acc.+ inf. 9; *quam, quālis, quantus, quī...* 10
extrēmus 'the last part (end) of' 33

F

fās n. indecl. 7
feminine place-names in *-us/-os* 7
fertur = nārrātur 18
fīlia, dat./abl. pl. *-ābus* 4
fore/futūrum (esse) ut 21
foret = esset 30
fungī + abl. 18

G

genitive: plur. *-um = -ōrum* 14, 24, 30; charge 24; description 4, 7, 8, 19, 21, 30; partitive 4, 19, 25; w. verbs: *taedet, paenitet* 10, *miserērī* 11, *damnāre* 24, *potīrī* 30, *rēfert* 31, *interest* 35; w. adj.s 8, 15, 21, 35; *meī, tuī...* 11, *suī* 27
gerund/gerundive: 20, *ad* + g. 14; *-und-* 24, 30
gerundive: w. *cūrāre* + acc. 4; g. + *esse* (fut. inf. pass.) 23; dat. 18, 20, 24
Greek names: endings 5, 7, 28

H

historic infinitive 19
historic present 6

I

ignārus + gen. 8
-illimus sup. 16
-im acc., *-ī* abl. 19
imperative: after *quīn* 11; fut. *mementō* 10
impersonal verbs: *praestat, iuvat* 8; *taedet, paenitet* 10; *cōnstat* 12, 24; *convenit* 12; *rēfert* 31; *interest* 35
impersonal passive of intransitive verbs 10, 21
indefinite pronouns 14
indirect command 27
indirect question 8, *ut...* 9
indirect discourse 18, 28
ineunte ... abl. abs. 33
īnfimus 'the bottom of' 4
infinitive, historic 19
inter-est (impers.) + *meā, tuā...,* gen. 35
i-stems: acc. *-im,* abl. *-ī* 19
iussū + gen. 12
iuvat (impers.) 8

L

late Latin 23, 32
locative (ablative) 4, 19, 32

M

magis, māximē + adj. 4
magnificus, comp. *-centior,* sup. *-centissimus* 4
medius 'the middle of' 4, 33
meī, gen. of *ego* 11
mementō fut. imp. 10
memor + gen. 8
-met 8

N

nātus + abl. (*orīginis*) 5
necesse est +. subj. 35
nom. + acc. 4, 12
nōscere nōvisse 27
numerals 23, distributive 26
nūptum (sup.) *dare* 21

O

oportet + subj. 35
opus esse + abl. 21

P

pae[...]c.+ gen./inf. 10
participle, perfect, of dep. verbs 14
partitive genitive 4, 19, 25
passive: *dīcitur, nārrātur* 4, *trāditur, fertur* 18
passive (impersonal) of intransitive verbs 10, 21
per- + adj./adv. 26
perfect ind. act. 3rd pers. pl. *~ēre* 14, 30
person: 2nd sg. pass. *-re = -ris* 7; 3rd pl. perf. ind. act. *~ēre = ~ērunt* 14, 30
person: 3rd pl. & 2nd sg. in general sense 12
placet + *ut* / acc. +inf. 23
plēnus + gen./abl. 6
pluperfect: pass. *~us fuerat* 23; subj. in indirect speech 28
plural 3rd pers. of people in general 12
poenās dare 7
pondō 24
postquam + perf. ind. 6
potēns + gen. 8
potential subjunctive (pres., imperf.) 12, 26
potīrī + abl. 7, gen. 30
prae-clārus, -potēns 26
praestat impers. 8
prefixes 29
present, historic, 6
prīmus 'the first part of' 7, 33
priusquam + subj. 15
purpose 9, 14

Q

quaesō 35
quālis, quam, quantus, quī... in exclamations 10
quam+sup./*prīmum* 18, 30-31
quantō... tantō +comp. 16

quārtō adv. = *quārtum* 32
quī- quae- quod-cumque 8
quī- quae- quod-libet 14
quīn adv. + imp. 11; *q. etiam* 11
quīn conj. + subj. 11
quīntō adv. = *quīntum* 32
quī- quae- quod-vis 14
quō... eō + comp. 16
quō + comp. + subj. (purpose) 27

R

-re = -ris: 2nd pers. sg. pass. 7
referre rem/dē rē 25
rē-fert (impers.) + *meā, tuā,* gen. 31
reflexive pron. 8
relative clauses: purpose 9, 14, 26; cause 9; result 14
rhetorical question 33

S

semideponent verbs 35
similis, sup. *-illimus* 16; + dat./gen. 15
simul atque + perf. ind. 6
solēre -itum semidep. 35
subjunctive: potential (pres., imperf.) 12
suffixes 31
suī, gen. of *sē* 27
summus 'the top of' 4
superlative: *māximē -eus/ -ius/-uus* 4; *-illimus* 16
supine I: 10, 14, 21
supine II: *mīrābile dictū* 9
syncopated forms 26

T

taedet +acc.+ gen./inf. 10
tantō + comp. 16
tense: historic pres. 6; *dum* + pres. 6; *postquam, ut, ubi, simul atque* + perf. 6
tertiō adv. = *tertium* 32
time, how long, *acc/abl* 32
timēre + dative 6
tuī, gen. of *tū* 11

U

ubi conj. + perf. ind. 6
-um = -ōrum 14, 24, 30
-und- ger. = *-end-* 24, 30
ut adv. (= *quōmodo*), in indirect question 9
ut conj. + perf. ind. 6
utī/utī = ut 14
utrī, utrīque plur. 16
utrimque 16

V

velle + subj. 34
vēn-īre (/*vēndere*) 4
ventum est (impers. pass.), 10, 21
verbal nouns (*~us*) 8, 12
vescī + abl. 7
vetus, sup. *veterrimus* 4